ROUTLEDGE LIBRARY EDITIONS: WW2

Volume 21

THE NEW ECONOMIC WARFARE

THE NEW ECONOMIC WARFARE

ANTONÍN BASCH

LONDON AND NEW YORK

This edition first published in 2022
by Routledge
2 Park Square, Milton Park, Abingdon, Oxon OX14 4RN

and by Routledge
605 Third Avenue, New York, NY 10158

Routledge is an imprint of the Taylor & Francis Group, an informa business

First published in 1942 by George Routledge & Sons, Ltd

All rights reserved. No part of this book may be reprinted or reproduced or utilised in any form or by any electronic, mechanical, or other means, now known or hereafter invented, including photocopying and recording, or in any information storage or retrieval system, without permission in writing from the publishers.

Trademark notice: Product or corporate names may be trademarks or registered trademarks, and are used only for identification and explanation without intent to infringe.

British Library Cataloguing in Publication Data
A catalogue record for this book is available from the British Library

ISBN: 978-1-03-201217-9 (Set)
ISBN: 978-1-00-319367-8 (Set) (ebk)
ISBN: 978-1-03-203576-5 (Volume 21) (hbk)
ISBN: 978-1-03-203578-9 (Volume 21) (pbk)
ISBN: 978-1-00-318802-5 (Volume 21) (ebk)

DOI: 10.4324/9781003188025

Publisher's Note
The publisher has gone to great lengths to ensure the quality of this reprint but points out that some imperfections in the original copies may be apparent.

Disclaimer
The publisher has made every effort to trace copyright holders and would welcome correspondence from those they have been unable to trace.

THE NEW ECONOMIC WARFARE

BY

ANTONÍN BASCH

LONDON:
GEORGE ROUTLEDGE & SONS, LTD
BROADWAY HOUSE : 68-74 CARTER LANE, E.C.4

First published, 1942

TO THE MEMORY OF MY MOTHER

THIS BOOK IS PRODUCED IN COMPLETE
CONFORMITY WITH THE AUTHORIZED
ECONOMY STANDARDS

PRINTED IN GREAT BRITAIN BY HEADLEY BROTHERS
109 KINGSWAY, LONDON, W.C.2; AND ASHFORD, KENT

CONTENTS

	PAGE
INTRODUCTION By Horace Taylor	vi
FOREWORD	ix
PUBLISHER'S NOTE	xi

1. THE ECONOMIC PREPARATION FOR WAR ... 1

    The Economic Causes of War—The Policy of Autarchy—Economic Aggression—Conquest by Foreign Trade

2. WAR ECONOMY ... 34

    Economic Impact of Total War—Organization of War Economy

3. THE WAR ECONOMIES OF GERMANY AND GREAT BRITAIN ... 58

    Germany—Great Britain—Defence Programme in the United States

4. ECONOMIC WARFARE ... 101

    Period up to the Defeat of France—After the French Armistice—The Present Situation

5. FROM WAR TO PEACE ... 123

    The War and the World Economy—The Totalitarian Plan for the "New Order"—The Democratic Programme—The Problem of Economic Democracy and Security—Reconstruction of Europe—Period of Transition

INDEX ... 153

INTRODUCTION

THERE are three general ways in which warfare and the economic life of nations are related. Firstly, there are the economic backgrounds out of which wars develop. These matters—imperialism, trade and financial discriminations, and international economic rivalries—have received much scholarly scrutiny in the period since 1918. The present study does not examine this already much-explored field. Secondly, there are the economic necessities involved in waging war. It is with these matters, defensive and offensive, basic and strategic, that this book is principally concerned. Thirdly, there are the economic aspirations which each of the two sides in international war seek to serve. Two patterns for economic life in the world at large, one as it will be if Germany and her Axis associates win the present war, the other as it will be if Britain and her allies win, are sketched in the final chapter of this study.

The economic necessities involved in waging war comprise a subject as old as warfare itself. But the arts of war always have advanced. Their progress in recent times has been so rapid and so far-reaching as to impose an unprecedented strain on the economic structure of a nation, and an unprecedented—life or death—responsibility on the people concerned. That, in brief, is the economic concomitance of "total" war. A nation's economic system must be articulated with the

Introduction

military needs of war; this involves great shifts of productive effort and important limitations of consumption. It also must be synchronized with military needs; the accelerated tempo of modern warfare calls for great speed on the economic front. In both respects economic factors are more acted upon than active.

One of the two means of co-ordinating economic effort and sacrifice with the needs of war is by subjecting all elements in a nation to the will of a dictatorial state. The other is by using the market and the price system as a means of securing the ends that are desired. The latter method, even when it is effective along productive lines, needs inevitably to be supplemented by direct restrictions on consumption. Both of these ways of securing the economic results that are needed are described in detail in this study. The first method is illustrated by the recent economic experience of Germany, the second by that of Great Britain. The defensive and offensive economic stratagems employed by both nations also are described and their effects analysed.

Dr. Antonin Basch, the author of this book, possesses unusual qualifications in training and experience for dealing with this subject. Few men of his scholarly capacities have had comparable opportunities to know at first hand the industrial and financial resources of the countries concerned, the qualities of their people, the strength of the attractive and repulsive forces that bear upon them, nationally and internationally. He was formerly Lecturer and Professor of Economics at the universities of Bratislava and Prague, and for a number of years was Director of Research of the Czechoslovak

National Bank. He was a representative of Czechoslovakia at the European Economic Conference at Stresa and at the World Economic Conferences at Geneva and London.

While this book contains much that will interest professional economists, Dr. Basch has sought above all else to make clear to people who are not technical experts the nature of economic warfare. The book is an expanded version of a series of six lectures on economic warfare delivered at Columbia during the Summer Session of 1941. The lectures, like the book, were not designed exclusively for specialists in the field of economics and they were attended by students and staff members from all parts of the university. The Department of Economics, under whose auspices the lectures were given, and the members of the university community who attended the lectures, are deeply indebted to Dr. Basch for the completeness and clarity with which he has treated a large and complicated subject. The publication of this book assures the promotion of understanding of this critically important subject among a still wider audience.

HORACE TAYLOR

Columbia University
1941

FOREWORD

THE present publication contains in extended and completed form a series of lectures delivered at Columbia University during the Summer Session of 1941. The main purpose of the series was to examine and illustrate the economic impact of a great modern total war, to outline the special preparation which such war involves, and to follow the transformation which the belligerent nations are compelled to adopt and which spreads to affect the entire world economy.

It was not, of course, possible in a work of this compass to develop a comprehensive theory of the economics of war, to analyse, especially, the problem of inflation as public expenditures absorb about 50 per cent of the national income, or, in particular, to examine in detail the special problems confronting the democratic countries. For these countries must determine how far they can achieve the necessary organization of their war economy without a thorough going system of compulsion.

The main part of the series (the manuscript was written for the most part before the German-Russian war began) was devoted to problems confronting the countries of Europe. But the principal lesson of the war has been the interrelation today of the whole world economy and the validity of the theses of collective security and an indivisible peace. The necessity has become apparent of providing in the future for a world organization to prevent any preparation of economic aggression which may pave the way for military aggression. I have been able only to outline some of these future problems as well as to point the present lessons.

The attempt of totalitarian powers to overcome the disadvantage of their lack of economic resources by thorough preparation and organization for war will not, I believe, succeed: the distribution of the world's wealth will not be permanently altered by conquest. Much of the wonder and mystery of these regimes will disappear and many old simple truths will again be appreciated. Europe will be the principal sufferer in a tremendous destruction of values. A new disciplined democracy, liberated from the egoism and opportunism of political parties and aware of the world's political, economic, and social interrelation, will face the constructive task of understanding and solving the world's economic and social problems. One of the chief products of the present war is certainly the clear knowledge that freedom and democracy can be maintained, granted that excess egoism and nationalism are overcome, only if it is defended with determination and a real willingness for sacrifice.

I am under special obligation to the Department of Economics of Columbia University for having invited me to deliver these lectures. Particularly I wish to express my most sincere thanks to the Chairman of the Department of Economics of Columbia University, Professor Horace Taylor, who encouraged me to publish

Foreword xi

this series of lectures and to whom I owe many valuable suggestions.

My sincere thanks are due to Miss Betty Moore, assistant in economics at Brown University, for her highly efficient help in the linguistic and secretarial preparation of the manuscript.

A.B.

New York
1941

PUBLISHER'S NOTE

THE Publishers regret that owing to war conditions it has been impossible to publish this book earlier. The author's manuscript was completed in the summer of 1941 in the U.S.A., and the book was published in New York in the early autumn of that year. Much has happened since then—especially the entry into the war of Japan and the U.S.A., and the 1942-43 Budget in this country—which would have made revision of this book desirable had not the author been so far away. None of these events, however, in any way invalidate the main theme and argument of the book, which in the Publisher's opinion are of such vital and permanent importance as to justify them in issuing the book in this country without further delay.

CHAPTER I

THE ECONOMIC PREPARATION FOR WAR

THE ECONOMIC CAUSES OF WAR

THE character of totalitarian war has changed to a great extent the relations between war and national economy which have prevailed for over a century. Understanding of this change is essential in the study of the economic causes of war, the economic impact of totalitarian war, and its economic and social consequences. Totalitarian war in its very nature demands the fullest efforts and sacrifices of the whole community, and there is no possibility of estimating its future effects on special sections of economic life or on particular economic interests. Therefore, a great modern war cannot be explained by theories which appeal to particular economic causes such as conflicts in foreign trade, or the interests of bankers, big business, and industry. Even the assignment of war profits as a motive cannot be taken seriously into consideration, despite the obvious efforts of the armaments industry everywhere to be on good terms with all national governments.

There are, of course, various theories which try to explain the present war mainly in terms of economic and social factors. The cause most commonly designated is the Versailles Peace Treaty, and especially its economic sections. No one could wish to pretend that the Versailles Treaty was a perfect work. It did, however, provide a general framework for a new world organization; there is no doubt that—despite the initial economic mistakes in its application—some suitable basis could have been discovered. This might well have been achieved if a new generation had been given time to carry out the treaty's principal ideas, and had been unhandicapped by all the repercussions of the war.

In any event, when the war menace became really very acute in 1938, the particular articles of the Treaty which had been most heavily attacked were no longer in force. They constitute no valid excuse for German policy.

In considering the importance of various economic and social forces in Germany, it is necessary to examine independently the years before 1933 and the period of the Nazi regime. After 1933 the initial steps were taken in preparation for the present catastrophe, first as indirect and then as direct economic mobilization and aggression. In view of the fact that there was only one great power which set up in peace time an organized war economy (under the name of defence) and kept steadily strengthening it during the six-year period, the future historian will not find it difficult to explain the last years leading up to the present war. The more important and difficult task will be to explain the origin and reasons for the Nazi regime, and then its success in Germany and abroad. This cannot be done without a thorough analysis of postwar economic and social policy, but a merely economic and social interpretation of Nazism would be overnarrow and misleading. Let us emphasize the following main features of this period: World economic equilibrium, based before 1914 fundamentally on the functioning of the British system had been destroyed, and no system organized in terms of international co-operation had taken its place. The adjustment of production to consumption in various parts of the world was never undertaken in a manner appropriate to the urgency of the situation. The problem of international debts and transfer was not organically settled; and foreign trade policy was not adjusted to the positions of creditor and debtor nations. The old truth—that only in an expanding world economy is it possible to achieve a step-by-step solution of critical points or bottlenecks—was not adequately recognized and adopted as a basis for action. In such a disorganized world order, the great difficulties of the German economy became even more serious. The success of a democratic policy in Germany depended on concerted international action. The post-war governments were not equal to this enormous task, and instead of initiating a real settlement of all such complicated problems they preferred mostly to follow the path of least resistance. I do not wish to speak of natural economic laws; it is sufficient to say that there are some basic principles and truths which are closely related to any national economy. It is impossible to disregard them permanently without creating a situation which leads certainly in the long run to severe crisis.

When, as the result of the structural dislocations of the world depression, the number of unemployed labour rose to thirty millions, it became urgent to assure to labour a greater degree of social and economic security—and that within the democratic organization. The political and social importance of this problem was not recognized in time, and its exploitation as an effective propaganda item was partly responsible for the Nazi success at home and abroad.

But the problem was not a purely German one. The general European economy, of which Germany is of course an important part, was not balanced after the war, nor was it adjusted to the changed world situation. A detailed analysis of this enormous complex may help to demonstrate the forces which made possible the Nazi victory. And this analysis involves problems far more complicated than those often brought forward as constituting causes of the war—namely, population pressure and the associated demand for living space. Hitler himself said to the Reichstag on April 28, 1939 : " It is intolerable that one nation should demand territorial expansion when there are less than fifteen inhabitants to the square kilometre, while other nations are forced to maintain 140, 150, or even 200 in the same area."

According to the German conception, the Reich should have 4 per cent of the world area, corresponding to its percentage of world population, whereas its actual territory is less than 0·5 per cent of world area. But the same disparity applies to most European states : the figures are for Poland, 1·6 per cent of world population and 0·3 per cent of world area ; for Czechoslovakia, 0·7 per cent and less than 0·2 per cent ; for Holland, 3·5 per cent and 1·5 per cent. Actually, it is the problem of all Europe, exclusive of Russia, and must be related to Europe's position in world production and world trade. For a long time it has been acknowledged that the Continent is relatively overcrowded (a problem which cannot be solved by war).[1] But it becomes difficult to accept this argument when at the same time the Third Reich supports an increasing birth rate, subsidizes marriages and large families, prohibits emigration, calls back German nationals from abroad, and as early as 1938 imports foreign workers to meet a labour shortage.

The demand for greater living space (*Lebensraum*) correlative with the thesis of over population has in the last few years been demonstrated to be only an attempt to conceal a political and strategic technique for dominating lesser powers. In asking for more living space, Germany asserted that " there are certain areas which by virtue of their geographical situation and economic resources, or it may be in virtue of historical association, are of special and perhaps exclusive interest to the Great

---

[1] See R. R. Kuczynski, *Living Space and Population Problems* (**Pamphlets on World Affairs**, No. 8, Oxford University Press, 1939), pp. 5, 8 ff.

Powers bordering on them. Those powers claim to enjoy a special economic position in their Lebensraum, and above all to take in them the measures necessary to their own strategic security ".[1] The real nature of the German living-space theory is clear from the fact that Germany included in its living space not thinly populated overseas countries, but the area of central and eastern Europe with overcrowded agricultural populations.

It is unnecessary to enlarge on the point that a larger living space can be gained in Europe only at the expense of other nations and by means of conquest and domination. Germany's claim—accepted by people who do not understand this particular problem—was simply an attempt to conceal her real purpose.[2] No such arguments are sufficient to explain even the economic background of this war. The whole picture should have become clear when the new regime immediately established a really aggressive economic policy.[3]

THE POLICY OF AUTARCHY

The organization of a new totalitarian Germany since 1933 marks the beginning of profound changes in Europe and virtually the end of efforts toward international economic co-operation. Germany was transformed into a planned and centrally administered economy, although the real purpose of the new programme was always concealed by party-sponsored explanations. It was clear,

[1] C. A. Macartney, *The Danubian Basin* (Pamphlets on World Affairs, No. 10, Oxford University Press, 1939), p. 28.

[2] "The plea for Lebensraum has often been the disguise for other sinister intentions." Lionel Robbins, *The Economic Causes of War* (Macmillan, London, 1940), p. 80.

[3] I do not think it correct to compare this with the Russian economic policy after the revolution. Russia's object was not an economy of the same high degree of development and the same vertical structure—it was not a transition, as in Germany, from a capitalistic to a totalitarian planned economy.

however, that international co-operation was a secondary consideration, and that the policy of autarchy reflected another very important element of the world's economy.

The aim of the policy was not an improved standard of living, although this was emphasized during the years of great unemployment. Rather the new regime established a real national defence economy—*Wehrwirtschaft*—with all other purposes subordinated to the ultimate goal of an impregnable military system. The leaders have thought and operated in terms of *Realwirtschaft* (real economy) instead of monetary economy. The unconditional priority of all processes important for national defence was plainly stated and systematically effected, regardless of costs and sacrifices. Such a policy means that despite increasing production and larger national income, per capita consumption should remain constant, or even, if necessary, decline. Within a centrally planned and administered economy, this can be achieved without great difficulty; it is illustrated to a certain extent by the first Russian five-year plan, which proposed to extend production of capital goods at the expense of goods for mass consumption. The motto " guns instead of butter "—not taken seriously abroad— was adopted by Germany without reservation, and was as fully carried out.

The war economy was only one manifestation of Germany's territorial ambitions. A complete plan for political and military expansion was developed, based on the experiences of the last war and projecting future military strategy. The function of *Wehrwirtschaft* was to render any possible blockade ineffectual. Hitler said, " All thoughts of a blockade against Germany may as well be buried now, for it is an entirely useless weapon."[1]

[1] To the Nazi Party Congress in Nürnberg, September 12, 1938; quoted from Hellmut von Rauschenplat and Hilda Monte, *How to Conquer Hitler* (Jarrolds, London, 1940), p. 26.

Before the outbreak of the war many features of the plan were concealed or even publicly denied. Usually it was argued that the economy of autarchy was forced upon Germany. After German military successes, however, prominent people there began to describe the preparation and operation of the programme. Let us quote some very interesting statements. In the January 1940 issue of *Der Vierjahresplan,* an official publication, M. Körner gave the following description of the general character of pre-war economic mobilization : " To turn the whole work and life of 80 million people toward war, to regulate the consumption of food and of important consumer goods, to direct factories and labour to meet the one central purpose, to distribute raw materials, and to solve a quantity of other questions is an unprecedented accomplishment in a national economy—the concentration of all economic forces upon the product which is thought most important in the fight for defence."[1] It is no doubt the best example in modern economic life of the organization of a whole national economy for several years with one primary purpose—preparedness for war.

The semi-official *Deutscher Volkswirt*[2] describes the building up of the programme : first, the final turning away from liberalism ; then the increase of domestic production under the first four-year plan ; next, the further increase of production for economic and military armament ; then at the end of 1938 a new task—national economic planning, which became necessary because of a shortage of labour and raw materials ; and, finally, the transformation of the entire organization for the actual conduct of a war. It is emphasized that " nothing was

---

[1] *Der Vierjahresplan* (January 5, 1940), p. 767.

[2] Hans W. Aust, " Dynamische Wirtschaftsführung," *Deutscher Volkswirt* (March 15, 1940), p. 767.

left to fortune. All was organized with consciously pledged determination, and well regulated and pushed forward ".

The leading member of the economic department of the German General Staff, W. Becker, wrote in 1940 in summarizing the effects of the defence economy : " Since 1933 German economic policy has been transformed from pure defence against the world economic crisis to the following of new national social and political aims, as well as to the creation of the Wehrwirtschaft which anticipated the total war blockade."[1]

It is not our task to describe the organization, the execution, and the results of the *Wehrwirtschaft* in Germany ; we shall limit ourselves to the main principles and achievements of the plan. Future history alone can show how it was possible to build up during a period of six years a complete economic military machine on a totalitarian pattern without any serious opposition from other great nations. It must have been widely known that the German economy was heavily dependent on raw material imports from democratic countries. A partial explanation may be the fact that a world believing in traditional economic principles underestimated the strength and the dynamic force of a seemingly static totalitarian economy.

As is well known, when the new regime started in Germany the huge reservoir of unemployed facilitated a rapid expansion of armament production ; this was followed by a great effort to achieve self-sufficiency in food supplies ; and finally a policy of almost complete autarchy was declared by Hitler in his speech of September 9, 1936 : " And to-day I hereby proclaim the new Four Year Programme as follows : Four years from now Germany must be entirely independent of foreign nations

[1] *Deutscher Volkswirt*, Supplement (March 25, 1940), p. 23.

with regard to all materials which can in one way or another be supplied by the German genius in our chemical and machine industries and in mining. The construction of this great new German raw materials industry will employ the masses who will become free after the conclusion of rearmament in a way that best serves the national economy."[1]

Thus Germany followed the full course of a policy of national self-sufficiency, regardless of costs of production, of prices of various commodities, and of relations with the world economy: foreign trade policy became only an instrument of the defence economy. Germany's economy became more and more separated from international economic relations, which were not considered of primary importance. Despite the later emphasis on the slogan " Germany must export or die ", the government was not prepared to change its autarchic course and return to full economic co-operation with other countries. Such an adjustment of the structure of German national economy was impossible within the Nazi organization. The policy of autarchy was considered useful and necessary to protect the country from the dangers of world economic crisis and war.

Germany's whole economic policy became independent of international considerations as far as possible—monetary and price relations were a more or less artificial link. The first large field of this policy was agriculture, where the new regime simply carried on and completed the protectionist programme inaugurated before the world crisis. The prices of agricultural products were regulated officially so as to become independent of all other price fluctuations. It was hoped that the farmers, guaranteed prices and markets, would increase production

[1] Hans Staudinger and Fritz Lehmann, "Germany's Economic Mobilization for War," *National Industrial Conference Board Economic Record* (July 24, 1940), p. 294.

as much as was necessary to secure self-sufficiency. Although it is difficult to obtain definite figures on Germany's success in this effort, and although opinions vary, nevertheless it can be assumed that Germany's food position was stronger in 1939 than in 1914.

Brandt estimates that Germany has attained a domestic food production adequate to 87 per cent of her needs[1]; other estimates go only to 83 per cent. There is, of course, a great deficiency in fat supply, of which only about 56 per cent was home produced (of 2,100,000 tons of animal consumption, only 1,200,000 tons were produced within Germany).[2] But all these estimates have to rely on many indirect sources. Furthermore, German capacity in this respect was underestimated because of incomplete documentation. (It is accordingly interesting to find that between 1933 and 1938, as a result of developing home production, the total supply of fats increased by 281,000 tons, but that the increase was not consumed.[3] In fact, the annual per capita consumption of fat fell from 58 pounds in 1932 to 55 pounds in 1937).[4] The estimate that total agricultural production has increased by 10 per cent since 1933 may not be inaccurate.[5] The fact must not be overlooked that large stocks of all kinds of foodstuffs had been collected before the outbreak of the war, and, as a matter of fact, the volume of these stocks was generally underestimated.

[1] Karl Brandt, "Foodstuffs and Raw Materials," in *War in Our Time*, ed. by H. Speier and A. Kähler (Norton, New York, 1939), p. 111.

[2] Rauschenplat and Monte, *op. cit.*, p. 29.

[3] *Nature*, CXLVI (December 21, 1940), p. 786.

[4] *Financial News* (Survey in "Germany's Bid for Self-Sufficiency,' a reprint of a series of articles, May, 1939), gives the following figures for self-sufficiency in agricultural products: wheat, 78 per cent of total consumption; rye, 97·4 per cent; barley, 93·4 per cent; eggs, 18·4 per cent.

[5] Werner Klatt, *Germany's Food in War and Peace* (Twentieth Century Fund, 1939), p. 702.

Achievements in industrial production were, of course, greater. The following figures are important. The entire industrial production of Germany (not including Austria and Czechoslovakia) was 28 per cent greater in 1939 than in 1913. With those two countries, the increase was perhaps 50 per cent.[1] The index of industrial production rose from 58 in 1932 to 125 in 1938,[2] that of producers' goods from 46 to 136 (195 per cent increase), and that of consumers' goods from 78 to 109 (39 per cent increase). Of course, various articles needed for armament—uniforms, automobiles, etc.—were included among consumers' goods.

The above figures show the trend of German development. It must be further considered that Germany in 1932 was already a highly industrialized country, in which the manufacturing equipment had been recently modernized with the help of foreign credits. This rapid expansion since 1933 has increased considerably Germany's share in world industrial production.

The increase of industrial production included a very thorough and comprehensive plan for all industries important for national defence—not only armament factories, but also all plants manufacturing raw materials or semi-finished goods for the armament industry. The authorities working out this programme relied on expert technical advice, and it is clear that German industry was fully co-operative. Thus a tremendous capacity was built up for meeting all direct and indirect needs of national defence. In the iron and steel, chemical, electro-technical, machine, rayon, cellulose, and other industries, basic capacity was extended. Reserve factories and even underground plants were established, regardless

---

[1] J. C. De Wilde, J. F. Green and H. J. Trueblood, "Europe's Economic War Potential," *Foreign Policy Reports* (October 15, 1939), p. 1398.

[2] *Wochenberichte des Instituts für Konjunkturforschung*, No. 8, 1939, p. 42.

of cost and economic need. Full preparation for war was the only decisive factor, and economic life had to conform.

But as an enormous capacity for war purposes was built up, the problem of raw materials became more and more important. Three distinct measures had been taken to remove this dangerous bottleneck: the use of all domestic resources of raw materials, the establishment of substitutes industries, and the accumulating of large reserve stocks. By means of the first, through the exploitation of hitherto unworked low-grade ores, output of iron ore was increased from 6,000,000 tons in 1935 to 10,900,000 in 1938; and, according to the plan of the Hermann Göring Werke, output should reach about 20,000,000 tons in 1941. Similar efforts, with less success, have been made with copper ore, lead ore, and so forth. The production of magnesium was greatly extended; and the 1939 output of aluminium was about 180,000 tons, despite the fact that the most important raw material —bauxite—had to be imported. In addition, fairly successful attempts were made to produce aluminium from domestic raw materials.[1]

A really great achievement from the technical point of view was the large-scale manufacturing of certain substitutes—of synthetic oil, rubber, textile fibres, and plastics. Although very few official statistics have been published (reporting statistical data on plants of military importance was forbidden after 1934), there are some indications regarding the volume of production at the beginning of the war. Synthetic oil production was 2,000,000 tons, or nearly one-third of peacetime consumption; synthetic rubber, about 30,000 tons; staple

---

[1] *Financial News* (May 1939), gives the following figures for production of minerals: iron ore, 27·5 per cent of German consumption; copper ore, 3·9 per cent; lead ore, 9·8 per cent; zinc ore, 64·3 per cent; magnesite, 17·5 per cent (with Austria, 141·7 per cent); petroleum, 10·9 per cent; pyrites, 21·4 per cent.

fibre about 200,000 tons, with production further increasing; the production of all plastics was very large, and their use was steadily widening. There is no doubt that synthetic production has been further extended during the war, and that new plants have been established also in Czechoslovakia and Austria.

It is clear that from the world-economy point of view the greater part of the production of substitutes is waste of labour and capital: for example, supplies of wood which took years to produce are used for staple fibre to replace annually maturing cotton, and coal and lime are made to take the place of natural rubber grown yearly. It must, of course, be conceded that these are high technical achievements, and that new uses of a permanent character will arise for some such products.

Generally the importance of the substitutes industry to the German war economy was underestimated abroad. For instance, the true role of plastics in the armaments industry was not recognized. Too much weight also was given to the difficulty of the high cost of production, which is not so significant in a totalitarian economy.

There were, of course, other limits to the whole tremendous programme of war activity in Germany, even before the war, set by the supply of labour, by German access to industrial raw materials, particularly coal, iron, and timber, and by transportation facilities. All these resources can be used for only one purpose, and the total productive capacity of a nation depends on the way in which they are related to one another. Just before the outbreak of war, it seemed that these limits had been reached: the working tempo slowed down, labour imports from abroad were intensified, female labour increased, and transport difficulties became more grave.

But economic planning for war had already given Germany a tremendous initial advantage. Not only had the German army obtained the most up-to-date equipment and accumulated great armament reserves, but the whole manufacturing machinery had been thoroughly organized to provide whatever was needed for war. And the stocks of all kinds of raw materials acquired since 1937 were greater than official statistics on production, consumption, and imports indicated. (Stocks of oil were later estimated at 6-8,000,000 tons. There were large stocks of metals and of all kinds of semi-finished goods needed for armament.)

Thus Germany started the war with her fighting forces fully equipped and her industry thoroughly organized in preparation for anticipated war needs and possible emergencies. To combine all that—to build a complete defence economy to a state of complete preparedness—was, of course, possible only within a totally new economic structure, a structure transformed from capitalism to an economy centrally planned and administered to achieve a single aim. Prices and wages were fixed and controlled ; production and labour were commandeered ; consumption of consumers' and producers' goods—civilian as well as military—was regulated and even rationed ; investments and the capital market were managed directly and indirectly ; foreign trade was completely regulated. Germany became detached from the world economy and devoted her fullest efforts to the achievement of the greatest possible self-sufficiency.

The well-known economic freedoms of the capitalistic economy were successively abandoned : prices and wages, labour, production and consumption, internal movements of capital. Price and market economy was rejected. (The promise of economic security made the new situation attractive to labour.) An economy static in its regulated single elements became dynamic under a central leadership. The greatest care was taken to manage German economy with regard to the achievement of the ultimate goal, and it is only fair to admit that Nazi Germany tried to benefit from all expert technical and economic advice, so far as it fitted into the general plan. Only the Russian economy can be compared with Germany's in regard to central planning and requisitioning. The fact that Germany accepted private property to a certain extent cannot be regarded as an essential difference between the German and the Soviet economic organizations.

Due mainly to this centrally planned and administered economy and to the already mentioned conception of the *Realwirtschaft*, the financing of the defence economy was carried out without the difficulties expected by those who ignored the new economic structure. The task was to canalize a considerable proportion of national income for war preparations. This proportion was officially stated for the period preceding the war at 90,000,000,000 reichsmarks, but certainly the expense to private industry resulting from the programme of self-sufficiency is not included here. Despite difficulties at various points, the financing was managed without any open currency inflation, or even a dangerous credit expansion. It cannot, of course, be said that the process was entirely voluntary. Receipts from taxes and customs duties increased from 6,647,000,000 reichsmarks in the fiscal year 1932-33 to 13,964,000,000 in 1937-38, and to 17-18,000,000,000 reichsmarks in 1938-39. The German national debt in 1933 was only 13,100,000,000 reichsmarks (due to the inflation and cancelling of reparation payments), and was estimated at the beginning of the war at 51,400,000,000 reichsmarks.[1] Thus the higher returns from taxes and the government's large borrowing on a controlled market provided the financial means for the

[1] *National Industrial Conference Board Economic Record* (July 24, 1940), p. 306.

execution of the whole programme. Germany started this period with an unorthodox and risky financial policy which could succeed only in a fully controlled economy with complete management not only of the capital market but of practically all national expenses. The taxation, borrowing, and other measures necessary for armament financing, together with price fixing and rationing, reduced purchasing power and prevented the beginning of inflation.

ECONOMIC AGGRESSION

The beginning of the economic war is to be dated at 1933, when, the new German economic policy having been established, that development which we shall call an "economic aggression" took place. In view of the enormous importance of war economy for actual warfare, it can be said that this development was the first step toward war. The expanding and autarchic character of the German totalitarian economy not only disturbed competitive cost economy, ruptured the natural price situation, and strengthened latent tendencies toward economic nationalism,[1] but it further aggravated the unbalanced social and economic position of Europe and the world generally. Knowing what unfortunate results the protectionist measures taken by large states have always had, we can see what influence the much more drastic German programme must have exercised on the whole situation in Europe.

And in consequence a great problem arose: how would the democratic states react, how would they face this economic aggression and approaching military danger? The question was whether democracies would be able to prepare for war while maintaining their basic

[1] Karl Brandt, "Foodstuffs and Raw Materials" in *War in Our Time* (ed. by Speier and Kähler), p. 123.

economic and political organization, or whether the only possibility for them was to follow the war economy pattern of the totalitarian states. The fatal unpreparedness of the democracies in recent history seems to confirm the second opinion. Kähler, for instance, says : " Dictatorships can achieve this balance—in armament—at a level which gives them an armament potential that democracies can hardly reach without serious social disturbances," and speaks of the " special armament capacity of dictated economies ". He rightly calls this problem a challenge to democracies to achieve that which may prove unattainable without vital changes in economic and social life.[1]

But the recently revealed fact of economic and military unpreparedness, although extremely grave, is not yet sufficient to prove the failure of the democratic system. History will have to examine why the democratic nations were so slow and shortsighted, and the reasons assigned for it will be as different as they will be fundamental. The question is whether democracies can prepare for total war in a time of military peace, and whether they can go so far as to ask even a considerable sacrifice for this purpose in the form of increased production and services and an attendant reduction in consumption. The process is certainly more difficult than in totalitarian states, because it involves securing the consent of the entire nation and convincing it that such sacrifices are necessary. If the process is started, however, and started in time, it can certainly be carried through, since to meet the demands of total war, the large democratic nations can call upon greater resources, greater flexibility, and greater freedom. The situation may have been similar to the armament race before 1914, but, if the democracies

[1] Alfred Kähler, " War Expenditures and Economic Balance," in *ibid.*, pp. 243, 244.

had begun their preparations earlier, they would have been taking an effective step against aggression. Of course, there is the further question of the relation between democracy and a controlled and planned economy, which we shall discuss more fully later.

For those who identify democracy with *laissez-faire* capitalism, it will be difficult to admit the possibility of a defence economy in a democratic regime. I hope this opinion is held by only a small minority. The question becomes: what are the peacetime limits to economic planning for defence by a democratic organization? The answer depends on the determination, unity, and discipline of the nation, the condition of the material and human resources and facilities making up its war potential, the extent of economic aggression by totalitarian states, and the timing of the defence policy. The success of the programme further depends on the size and strength of the state. Small states will be unable to bear the heavy burden and necessary sacrifices over a long period of time —not because of their democratic character, but because of their relatively weak economic and military positions in total war.

There can be no doubt that democratic states could achieve strong, efficient defence economies without giving up the basis of either their economic or their political organization. Much that is actually the result of temporary maladjustment is blamed on the democratic system. It is possible within the framework of a democratic state to organize (and if necessary subsidize) various important war industries, or even build shadow (reserve) factories, to train skilled labour, to acquire large stocks of various commodities, to prepare all the details of economic mobilization, and so forth. These are problems of organization requiring planning, discipline, and determination, but not the suspension of the democratic regime; and failure to solve them does not prove the essential incapacity of democracy.

The tragic fact remains that the great democratic nations did not recognize and evaluate the real character and danger of German economic aggression, and accordingly did not mobilize their resources to meet the situation. They were too faithful to the French theory, which emphasized the necessity for future strength in economic war potential rather than the immediate mobilization of it. Even so, because they possessed initially superior war potentials, the democracies were not forced into the policy of self-sufficiency and of defence economy in the German sense, but could attend more to the development of the armament industry itself, including all goods and equipment required for a modern war. The greatest *potential de guerre* is of no use, however, if an enemy superior in speed and efficiency of action secures the victory before this potential can become really effective.[1]

Both Great Britain and France, as budget expenditures show, began large-scale preparations for defence only in 1938.[2] John Maynard Keynes suggested in August 1938

[1] H. Hellmer, "Effektiv siegt über Potential," *Deutscher Volkswirt* (June 28, 1940), p. 1362.

[2] James Frederick Green, *Economic Mobilization of Great Britain Foreign Policy Report* (July 1, 1939): Defence expenditures, according to the British budget, were

1935	137 million pounds
1936	186 million pounds
1937	262 million pounds
1938	400 million pounds

In the whole-year period the budget's defence provisions were 985 million pounds. German defence expenditures for the same four years amounted to at least 5 or 6 billion pounds. The budget for 1939 contained defence appropriations of 630 million pounds, estimated at 12 per cent of national income; Germany in the same year spent 2-2½ billion pounds, or 30-35 per cent of German national income.

France, according to the budget, spent 74 billion francs (10 billion marks) for defence between 1934 and the first half of 1939; that is a small fraction of German expenditures in the same period.

that the government accumulate and carry over permanently £500,000,000 worth of goods, at an annual cost of about £20,000,000. And it was not until July 1939 that Great Britain created a special Ministry of Supply for the purpose of hastening economic mobilization, and of effecting some kind of planning and administration in this section of national economy without destroying basic democratic principles. More specifically, the Ministry was to secure priority for government orders, to requisition when necessary the output of certain industries, to examine records and fix prices in disputes between industry and the government, to provide storage facilities, and so forth.

France was relying on natural resources even more heavily than Great Britain. A plan for economic mobilization had been worked out, but little was done in the preparatory period to bring it into effective operation. Only after Munich, and still more clearly after the German occupation of Prague, did France recognize the necessity for speeding up; by June 1939 estimated military appropriations for that year exceeded 50 billion francs, or one-fifth of the accepted figure for the French national income.[1]

The French Parliament adopted a law promulgated July 11, 1938, granting the government sweeping powers for mobilization of the nation's resources in time of war and authorizing it to undertake peacetime planning for war needs. This law served as the basis for many decrees proclaimed by the French Cabinet after it assumed emergency powers on March 19, 1939. But it was obvious that these measures could not cancel the time handicap.

Of course, economic and military defence preparations were considered necessary by many states of central and

[1] David H. Popper, "The French War Economy," *National Economic Conference Board Economic Record* (July 24, 1940), p. 313.

eastern Europe, which felt themselves especially menaced by Germany's expansion. As already pointed out, the situation of smaller states in modern warfare is unusually difficult because of the lack of natural resources, the more severe effects of the war burden on public finances, and so forth. Czechoslovakia can be taken as an example of one such country which was trying to make defence preparations. She had, by even Germany's admission, done everything possible to meet the imminent danger—to achieve a strong defence without abandonment of the democratic system. The Czechs were fully aware that the work must begin in peacetime. A special law on May 13, 1936, authorized the government to take all military and other measures, including planned exploitation of economic and political forces, necessary to protect the nation against aggression. A Supreme Council for National Defence was established to plan economic mobilization in the production, distribution, and consumption of goods.[1] Another section of the same law gave the government wide powers in connection with industrial production.[2] These measures permitted Czechoslovakia to make large-scale preparations and, despite a few extraordinary steps dictated by the emergency, to retain democratic control.

[1] The following tasks were specifically mentioned: to assure production of agricultural and industrial goods as well as supplies of raw materials, to provide an adequate food supply for the armed forces and civilian population, to issue directions for the allocation of labour, and to determine the financial measures necessary in an emergency, including the principles of price policy.

[2] Industrial enterprises important for national defence were required to give information regarding their equipment, production, supply of raw materials, and the possibility of shifting from peace to war production; they could be compelled to keep a prescribed stock of raw materials. A specially designated group of "registered enterprises" could be ordered to adapt their technical equipment to enable them to increase production in an emergency, as well as to move plants to points selected by military authorities, and to change and extend their production. A detailed programme for national defence was thus prepared.

The effects of far-reaching and continued defence preparations were clearly evident in Czechoslovakia. Over a period of years, they come to exert heavy pressure on the democratic institutions of a small state ; increasing sacrifices generate friction and menace economic equilibrium in a manner not unlike that of actual warfare. The individual measures are less important than the extent and duration of the whole programme, and that is dictated by pressure from the great totalitarian defence economies.

A similar situation developed in other European countries. The shadow of war hung over economic life. Armament production was pushed, new plants were built, and even in small countries the policy of self-sufficiency in strategical commodities was adopted. " Strategically safe " areas were designated, to which old industries were transferred, and in which new industries were established. Output was increased, capacity enlarged, and reserve (shadow) factories were constructed. Everywhere, along with high industrial activity and an apparent economic recovery, went growing financial burdens. Such was the trend in Czechoslovakia, Poland, Hungary,[1] Yugoslavia, and Rumania, and also in Belgium and Switzerland. Italy, of course, as a totalitarian country, pursued even more vigorously the policy of self-sufficiency and defence, but never reached the German level of efficiency.

Thus the financial, economic, and social situations changed everywhere in Europe under the pressure of Germany's totalitarian and aggressive policy. The fact of high business activity originating in defence production could not conceal the fundamental deterioration of the whole situation, with a steadily increasing portion of national income allocated to armament and other

[1] Hungary promoted more than other countries, although with no more valid economic grounds, the policies of autarchy and artificial industrialization.

unproductive purposes, and with increasing state intervention in the national economy. And it became more and more clear that conditions in smaller countries could not continue for long without profound changes in their whole political and social organization. The widening influence of Germany's foreign trade and exchange control contributed to the general instability.

CONQUEST BY FOREIGN TRADE

Germany's foreign trade and foreign exchange policy, as an integrated part of her whole system, served to strengthen the defence economy and to expand the living space claimed by Nazi theorists. Her position as a debtor country, as well as the situation created in other nations by their own agricultural and raw material crises and by the international financial collapse, was very skilfully exploited. Foreign trade and exchange were, of course, subjected to complete control, to a commandeering directed from a central agency for the achievement of a definite purpose. There is no essential difference between Germany's centrally directed foreign trade and Russia's foreign trade monopoly; the latter is carried on by government agencies, and the former by private business according to government instructions. Following this method, Germany detached its price level from that of the international market, and so introduced different systems for domestic and foreign trade.

The object of German trade policy was not to increase the exchange of commodities in such measure as the expanding international division of production permitted and thus ultimately to raise the standard of living. Instead, the self-sufficiency idea was dominant: exports were encouraged in order that raw materials and other commodities needed for national defence might be imported. Whereas both national income and the total volume of production increased considerably between 1933 and 1939, the figures for German imports and exports did not show the same trend.[1] The figures contrast sharply with the government's repeated statements that efforts to revive foreign trade were being made. In point of fact, the same general plan of foreign trade was followed in each of two spheres—one between Germany and free-trade countries, and the other between Germany and countries using clearing and barter agreements. In the latter sphere fell most of the countries of central and eastern Europe, which Germany claimed as part of her living space. The German policy of control is an excellent example of what can be accomplished by planned trade in a world unaware of its real purpose and thus not sufficiently determined or united to oppose it. More than at any previous time this commandeered foreign trade became a powerful weapon of economic and political penetration.

The plan was to purchase from countries where Germany was forced to pay in foreign exchange only those commodities which she could not buy in the so-called "clearing" states. In this way the supply of foreign exchange was saved to finance rearmament. "Clearing agreements took the place of individual payments between exporters and importers, payment through the collective account settling the balance of the entire foreign trade."[2]

[1] Germany's foreign trade in billions of reichsmarks (1938 figures include Austrian trade):

	Imports	Exports
1933	4·14	4·75
1934	4·45	4·17
1935	4·16	4·27
1936	4·21	4·76
1937	5·46	5·91
1938	6·05	5·62

[2] S. Antonin Basch, "Conquest by Foreign Trade," in *Trusts and Estates* (New York, April 1941), pp. 347, 351.

After Germany had attained a firm position in many of the European and overseas countries through her barter and clearing agreements, she went a step farther and announced a new plan for foreign trade. This, sometimes called the "Schacht Plan", was a truly totalitarian trade policy. It stated openly that only imports of foodstuffs and raw materials would be permitted (all imports were brought into a license system), and that exports would consist mainly of finished products. Germany exerted every effort to force this plan on other countries, and was able to influence directly the structure of their foreign trade, and indirectly even their production.

The problem of the relation *between free-trade countries and states with controlled foreign trade* came to present many difficulties. Foreign countries were to adapt themselves as best they could to the needs of Germany, calculated in terms of the Nazi economy alone. Various states endeavoured, with more or less success, to repel this attack. The position of the free-trade country was relatively weakest, and the greater their trade with Germany the more seriously were they affected. Some attempted a counter attack using the same weapon —export and import controls. They were only partly successful; the fact that they were small countries (the great democracies did not use these counter measures) meant that they had much less bargaining power than Germany. There was also a great deal of pressure within these states from the exporters, whose products Germany offered to take at higher prices. It was difficult, further, to reconcile private interests which clashed when the exports of one group were restricted so as to favour another. Finally, we must not forget that financial creditors of Germany were demanding the admission of German exports by their countries. As a whole, the Nazi programme was successful, and even great powers were induced to trade on German terms ; this is indicated by the change in the structure of Germany's imports, which took place according to plan.[1]

Despite the higher level of prices in Germany (on the basis of the official exchange rate of the reichsmark) it was possible to export when necessary at prices substantially lower than those of foreign competitors. This was sheer dumping. Restitution of the difference in prices was made to the producers through a common fund secretly collected—a so-called export tax paid by all enterprises, which amounted to many millions of marks yearly. This system permits extensive dumping. Whereas the limit to such dumping when used by a private concern or cartel is the profit margin which the industry in question can get in the domestic market, there is no such limit in a totalitarian economy. It is no longer a question of what the exporting industry is receiving through domestic sales, but of how the burden of the taxes destined to compensate the losses of exporting industries is to be distributed through the whole economy, and of what the final effects of this procedure may be. Therefore, for a totalitarian economy in which foreign trade represents only a relatively small part of total trade, there will be practically no normal limits to dumping. Definite limits always exist in theory, but actually it can go on as long as the totalitarian organization of production and distribution can be maintained.[2]

German foreign trade, except perhaps for products

---

[1] The result of this system of control is indicated by a comparison of the decline in volume of each of the several categories of imports from 1926-30 to 1934-38. Thus, total imports declined 22 per cent, foodstuffs 27 per cent, finished industrial products 54 per cent, semi-finished products 17 per cent, and raw materials only 3 per cent. Staudinger and Lehmann, *op. cit.*, p. 304.

[2] It was estimated that in the last years before the war, all export subsidies amounted to one-third of total exports, that is, 1,400,000,000 reichsmarks or less than 2 per cent of national income.

regulated by strong international cartels, became an uncertain and disturbing element in the world market. A special kind of foreign trade expansion was undertaken in connection with the agricultural countries of central and eastern Europe, where Germany made full use of a difficult situation. This part of Europe had always been claimed as an area of special German interest; under the expansive tendencies of the autarchic totalitarian economy it came to be considered " living space ". Such countries could provide no outlet for German population : Hungary, Rumania, Yugoslavia, Bulgaria, Greece, Turkey, and to a certain extent Poland, Austria, and Czechoslovakia had an overcrowded agricultural population. It was rather a question of economic exploitation, of including this territory in Germany's Great Economy (*Grossraumwirtschaft*). In plain terms, Germany wanted to strengthen her own economic war potential by annexing adjacent areas and securing access to their resources, especially foodstuffs, oil, and some important minerals.

Germany understood the situation better than the western countries, despite the fact that the League of Nations Conference in Stresa in 1932 produced a clear analysis of the reasons for and nature of the central and eastern European crisis. Conditions had grown steadily worse after the general stopping and withdrawal of foreign credits and after the fall in agricultural prices. In terms of the world economy, the Stresa estimates of necessary export outlets for these countries were not unreasonable, and the suggested measures regarding the financial crisis and the problem of debt transfer were not impossible of execution.[1] The primary need was for the

[1] The Stresa Conference proposed to make possible (if necessary, to subsidize) exportation of the following agricultural products from central and eastern Europe : 1,600,000 tons of wheat, 1,500,000 tons of barley for fodder, 1,350,000 tons of corn, 400,000 tons of rye, 300,000 tons of barley for brewing, and 100,000 tons of oats. These were very small quantities compared with the exports of overseas countries.

western European countries to buy quickly and prevent a further decline of business activity.

The situation presented to Germany an excellent opportunity to establish closer ties with those nations and at the same time to alleviate the difficulties of her own foreign exchange position. She began large purchasing, using clearing and barter agreements. In the beginning, the countries of central and south-eastern Europe welcomed Germany's plan as a means of mitigating the export crisis; they did not concern themselves, at first, with the problem of how the exports to Germany would eventually be paid for. Exporters frequently received prices considerably higher than those prevailing in the international market, and they believed that clearing agreements would enable them to receive payment without difficulty. (It has already been shown that the framework of general economic control permits payment of higher prices for imported goods if this is considered desirable.) The consequences of this development soon became evident. As a result of mass purchases, Germany became the debtor of these countries, some of which acquired considerable credit balances in the clearing accounts. The higher prices paid by the Germans raised the entire price level in central and south-eastern Europe, were an obstacle to the adaptation of prices to the world level and, in this way, made it increasingly difficult for the so-called " clearing " states of these parts of Europe to export to other countries than Germany—thus bringing them closer to the German economy.

The exporters, thinking only of their immediate interests, urged the governments and the National banks of their countries to make it possible for them to export to Germany in spite of the unfavourable state of the clearing accounts, and demanded that the central banks of issue see to it that immediate payment be made for the exports without taking into consideration the state of the collective account with Germany. The central banks, forced to advance loans, sometimes even at the risk of credit inflation, sought means of maintaining this way of trading. They had to adopt such measures as forcing importers to make still further purchases from Germany instead of from other countries, and in this way acquiring payment for exporters to Germany. Importers, applying for foreign exchange to cover imports from abroad, were often forced to buy in Germany, sometimes at higher prices for goods of poorer quality. Thus Germany, who had first become a debtor as the result of her mass imports, enjoyed a considerable enlargement of the volume of her trade with the majority of these countries. At the same time she obtained in this manner a certain degree of control over the economic policy of these countries. By inflating prices she divorced their price levels from the world market system, and, finally, reached the position of being able to dictate foreign exchange rates favourable to herself. Thus in connection with the Schacht Plan a change took place in the structure of the trade of the countries of central and south-eastern Europe with Germany and resulted in a change in the structure of production.

Germany continued to strengthen her position and brought still greater pressure to bear. Once a sufficient degree of control was achieved, Germany began to take a hand even in internal policies, giving preference to exporters and importers sympathetic with the Nazi regime. The systematic application of these methods of foreign trade brought impressive results. From 1935 to 1937 Germany's exports to the countries of central and south-eastern Europe increased by 62 per cent, while her total exports increased by only 38 per cent. German imports from these countries increased by 54 per cent while total German imports increased by only 30 per cent.[1] In general, the smaller the country dealing independently with Germany, the less complete was its control over foreign trade; furthermore, the more conflicting the interests among various groups of producers and exporters, the more successfully could Germany gain complete influence.[2]

Repeated efforts were made to emancipate the trade of these countries from the excessive and unnatural influence of Germany. France, England, Czechoslovakia, and other nations were called upon to increase their purchases in the states of central and eastern Europe and thus to defend their political positions. One serious effort was represented in the organization of the economic Little Entente, which was based on the belief that economic stabilization and permanent recovery in these countries was possible only if general business activity increased and if new industries, for which suitable production and consumption possibilities existed, were systematically created. It was recognized both that production of foodstuffs and raw materials would not be sufficient to raise the level of living in central and south-eastern Europe and that these areas represented the

---

[1] In 1937, imports from Germany reached 29 per cent of Rumania's total imports, 26·2 per cent of Hungary's, 32·4 per cent of Yugoslavia's, 59·8 per cent of Bulgaria's; Germany took 19·6 per cent of Rumania's total exports, 24·1 per cent of Hungary's, 21·7 per cent of Yugoslavia's, and 43·1 per cent of Bulgaria's.

German imports from Balkan and Mediterranean countries rose from 10·9 per cent of total German imports in 1929 to 20·2 per cent in 1938. Staudinger and Lehmann, *op. cit.*, p. 305.

[2] A leading authority on German foreign trade policy, Carl Ritter, wrote in the *Deutscher Volkswirt* (December 20, 1940), p. 42, explaining the trading drive in this area, very significantly as follows: German sacrifices consisted in paying for agricultural products from the Danubian Basin prices higher than those current in the world market. The improvement and welfare of national economy in the Danubian countries is dependent upon the improvement of Germany's economic position. Only a great and powerful Germany can guarantee economic well-being for those countries.

last large reserve of potential purchasing power which remained to be developed. The Little Entente achieved a remarkable degree of success but was of course disturbed permanently by the German counter activity, by the difficulty in exporting great quantities of agricultural products to Czechoslovakia, and by the lack of co-operation of the western countries. For instance, the Czechoslovakian plan to balance German pressure by creating a co-operative organization for the export of cereals and other products to the markets of western European countries was killed by the failure of the latter to understand and assist.[1]

The German plan of economic penetration was definitely successful after the invasion of Austria and Czechoslovakia. Both these countries had held important positions in the industry and banking of the Danubian states—positions which Germany could now take over. She acquired large foreign trade possibilities with the former markets of both countries, and absorbed then more than 50 per cent of the foreign trade of all Danubian states. Full economic control had been attained.

The economic treaty concluded with Rumania on March 23, 1939, is an excellent illustration. Germany asked a complete moulding of Rumanian economy to fit German needs. A long-range programme under German supervision was to make Rumania's economy supplementary to Germany's. Germany was given extensive privileges for the exploitation of Rumania's natural resources. She was to establish various organizations which in fact would enjoy extra-territoriality. Germany assured for herself the lion's share of Rumanian exports of oil and other essential raw materials and foodstuffs. The exchange ratio was changed in favour of the

[1] S. Antonin Basch, *The Reagrarization of Europe and the Economic Crisis of the Danubian States* (in Czech). Prague, 1934.

reichsmark. This kind of agreement was the forerunner of the reduction of central and south-eastern European countries to a semi-colonial status.[1]

Thus Germany used the new weapon of penetration through the drive of organized trade to secure a firm ascendancy in all of central and south-eastern Europe, cutting off this territory from other markets by monetary and price policy and forcing it into economic dependence, She thus constructed in effect a great economic bloc, which worked with her in a close relation.

As a general result of the German foreign trade policy, the following development became clear: Complete control of foreign trade by a great power, highly developed and in close connection with the world economy, tended to reduce the general volume of international trade and led to an extension of control to other fields of national economy and to an increase in the number of states which were compelled in self-interest to follow the same course. It may further result in the formation of larger economic units wherever that is possible, since such units constitute for smaller nations their only appropriate means of self-defence.

The totalitarian defence economy, combined with foreign trade measures looking to conquest, exercised a profound influence everywhere, but the primary impact was on Europe. For here the Nazis' desire to exploit and dominate other countries became more and more evident and their official statements more and more unconvincing —being obvious propaganda efforts which did not merit serious discussion.[2]

The importance of such economic and technical preparations for the actual carrying on of totalitarian war

---

[1] Paul Einzig, *World Finance, 1939-1940* (Kegan Paul, London, 1940), p. 77.

[2] Lionel Robbins, *The Economic Causes of War*, p. 85 : " The economic motives of totalitarian powers are the motives of barbarian hordes."

clearly rendered necessary a change in the concept of aggression entertained by the League of Nations—although this need was neither understood nor answered. The proper time for stopping an aggression by a large power is when it begins, at least when that aggression takes at first, as did the German, an economic form. With that moment a modern war is under way, and the conception of collective security must be extended to include common action to check such economic aggression. It would have been easy to stop Germany, even later, had a determined and united effort been exerted by the democratic states to force her to cease her measures of war economy. Lack of unity and imagination and false hopes of appeasement and compromise between the totalitarian and the free economies prevented such co-ordinated action. And the great powers failed to develop the alternative check that might have been afforded by large-scale preparations for national defence.

In the absence of a united procedure the European economy by 1938 faced increasing difficulties and growing tension. The shadow of war became an obstacle to any economic consolidation, the crisis became steadily more imminent, and after 1937 the question became very real whether and how it might be possible to transform the German economy from a war to a peacetime basis without upsetting the entire economic balance of Europe, It was clear that this could be done only through very large-scale international economic co-operation, with Germany both able and willing to return to a free economy and to abandon the objective of defence for that of welfare. In spite of the fact that the United States, Great Britain and France were prepared to initiate and support this action to the full, the period of economic warfare was followed—as the pattern of totalitarian aggression requires—by direct military action.

Chapter II

WAR ECONOMY

ECONOMIC IMPACT OF TOTAL WAR

THE economic impact of total war between great nations with a developed national economy is of such proportions and intensity as to interfere with all items of economic life. For it transforms peace economy into war economy, of which the one prevailing purpose is support of actual military warfare. Economic forces and adjustments have steadily assumed a more important role in the great wars of the twentieth century. The nature of modern total war has minimized the distinction between the fighting forces and civilian population.[1]

The single task of the war economy takes both a constructive and a destructive form. It involves, on the constructive side, supplying the fighting forces with the maximum of goods and services in the shortest possible time. In this effort it must, to the fullest possible degree, preserve justice in the distribution of sacrifices and avoid economic dislocation and disruptions which may impede the post-war reconstruction. In its destructive phase—which is economic warfare proper—it must weaken and damage as much as possible the potential and active economic strength of the enemy. It is obvious then that economic considerations such as the profit motive, competition, market price laws, and private economic sovereignty must be subordinated to the nation's primary aim.

Within the limits set by the available human and

---

[1] " Whether fighting, working, or contributing capital, everyone has to bring forward every bit of reserve to help the nation toward victory." Carl Joachim Friedrich, " Totalitarian War," in *Plan Age* (May 1940), p. 162.

material resources, the dimensions of the efforts and sacrifices which the nation must make are dictated by the intensity of the aggressor's war effort. In this relationship the factors of time and of preparedness are of great importance. The essential structure of war economy is the same in totalitarian and in democratic countries, and inherent in all are certain common principles of function. In the modern war economy we must part with traditional monetary conceptions and consider the terms of real economy. Such procedure makes more clear the importance of the war economy's structure and operation.

This becomes more evident when we examine the basic possibilities and limits of a nation's economic efforts, or when we speak, using Pigou's term, of the " real war fund ".[1] Economic possibilities are limited on the credit side by the maximum output of goods and services. Since there is clearly a great difference between developed and undeveloped resources, we cannot be satisfied with a general account of the economic war potentials of various nations ; beyond that it is important to determine the extent to which production has been directed toward war, and, finally, how efficiently and comprehensively it has been organized.

I think that we shall have a clearer picture of the real war fund if we consider total national production as the basic item. To the new production we must add the volume of existing stocks of all kinds ; this is again the question of economic preparation for war. The demands of total war are of such dimensions that, in my opinion,

[1] A. C. Pigou indicates four principal sources of the real war fund : (a) augmented production, (b) reduced personal consumption, (c) reduced investment in new forms of capital, and (d) depletion of existing capital. From *The Political Economy of War* (Macmillan, London, 1941), p. 30.

A German writer, R. M. Hettlage, describes this fund as follows : augmented production of goods important for war through increased work, increased consumption of existing real commodities, vast reduction of total consumption, and reduction of new formation of real capital. From *Deutscher Volkswirt* (December 20, 1940), p. 475.

they cannot be satisfied for a longer period of time from increased production alone. This means that the other items in the economic balance must be altered and adjusted, and that consumption in the largest sense must be reduced. As long as only normal civilian consumption is curtailed, expenses of the war are met out of income; but when it becomes necessary to stop renewing or maintaining producers' equipment, the costs of war are paid out of the national substance. The case is similar where existing stocks are consumed without being replenished.

A great war involves simultaneous efforts to increase production and to reduce consumption. How far consumption must be reduced depends upon various circumstances—the available resources, old stocks, state of preparedness, momentum of the war, etc. But the longer a nation puts off this necessary effort, the longer the war may last, with proportionately greater sacrifices at the end.

Before taking up the question of resources supplied by foreign countries, one further point should be mentioned. The opinion has been expressed that it may be possible to satisfy war demands by increased production without curtailing existing consumption. Quite apart from technical difficulties I find this view unacceptable. War requirements are too urgent and too vast to be thus satisfied, even in an economy with large resources. They involve a profound adjustment of the civilian population. In other words, a great total war tends inherently to depress the level of living of the fighting nations.[1] The opposite problem arises—that of finding the limits to the

[1] There is no contradiction to this statement for instance in the situation of Canada, where in the past fiscal year the national income was $1,200,000,000,000 larger than before the war, while the increase in the outlays caused by the war was about $1,000,000,000,000. Canada could not be regarded as a country highly developed economically nor —due to the total situation—were her efforts at this time, although great, adequate to a total war in the proper sense as in the case of Great Britain.

reduction of civilian consumption and the depletion of the national substance. Nor can a definite inclusive answer be given : the point at which exhaustion begins and makes itself felt differs according to national customs and endurance.

The general effect of war economy upon the nation becomes clear if we view it in terms of real or natural economy. When the state requisitions goods and services, the sacrifices and burdens borne by its citizens are made evident. All other procedures are made secondary to the priority of war requirements. The standard of living can be raised only at the expense of armament production ; it is impossible to have both more guns and more butter. The members of the community come to recognize that they must work harder to manufacture and deliver goods without any corresponding economic return. Phrasing the matter in these terms also makes it clear that war requirements must be satisfied out of current production and existing stocks, and cannot be put off upon a future generation. When the war is over, the depletion of real capital is not concealed by accumulated financial claims.

The real war fund can be increased by supplies from abroad, whether in the form of foreign goods bought against cash payment or on credit, or in the form of voluntary contributions, or in the form of conquest and contributions based on it. All these procedures for supplementing war resources are important in the present war and are illustrated in the British and German war economies. The British economy appears much weaker than the German if we take into account the resources of Great Britain alone. Her industrial and agricultural capacity is far below that of Germany, and her population is only 47,000,000, in contrast to the 70-80,000,000 in Germany proper and the 100,000,000 in so-called

Greater Germany. Again, Germany has the advantage of incomparably greater stocks of armament and of a war economy whose organization is nearly complete. Finally, Germany's real war fund has been tremendously augmented by lucrative military conquests. But we must take into account Great Britain's ability to increase her war fund from abroad, using for this purpose gold, foreign exchange, and other accumulated foreign assets. She may also rely upon large contributions by members of the British Commonwealth and the Lend-Lease aid of the United States. This illustrates the extent of the struggle in which the two countries are engaged.

As has already been stated, there are certain principles of war economy which obtain for every type of economic system and every form of government. It is evident that a general economic plan, an economic strategy, is always essential. In totalitarian Germany and communist Russia organized planning is used even in peacetime; in democratic countries like Great Britain, which possess a free economy, the position of a planned war economy constitutes a real problem. The special problem here merges with the general problem of the relation between free and planned economies.

Since we are to consider the question in a later chapter I shall limit myself here to one brief remark. It is often said that a democratic form of government admits only of a capitalistic economic system. I myself do not accept this identification, but even if it is granted, the further question arises whether capitalistic economies can operate in wartime efficiently enough to fulfil all war requirements. As we have seen, the one real purpose of the war economy is to develop the real war fund to the fullest possible extent. Is there reason to hope that the war fund can be essentially augmented through the functioning of price mechanisms and the profit motive?

In plain terms, we must answer that the possibility of adjustment in already developed national economies is slight. On the contrary, a free price system would slow down the necessary economic organization, cause various dislocations including social unrest, and hamper efforts toward greater efficiency of the whole economy. After all, can a free market economy be admitted in a period in which there is no freely competitive market and in which war expenditures reach 40-50 per cent of the national income? In the commodity, capital, or labour markets, the requirements imposed by government are absolutely decisive, determining prices, rates on interest, and wages. The position of the state in time of war can be compared with that of an all-comprehensive monopoly. Monopolistic price theory may be applied in determining optimum prices and other conditions under which the national economy would best meet the war requirements. For the main task of the war economy is to attain a maximum efficiency in production and distribution.

Obviously, in a democratic regime also, the state's field of activity will be greatly enlarged and interference with private economy will be extended. But even in democratic countries the introduction of planning and central control in times of emergency does not mean a final change in the regime. For it is clear, first, that the organization is only a temporary product of national emergency, and, second, that basic political rights and the democratic controls exercised, for instance, by the British Parliament, by public opinion, and the press remain in full power.[1] To what extent the state must

---

[1] Marriner S. Eccles, speaking of the situation in the United States, said: "Democracy and the system of free enterprise can function to provide reasonably full and sustained employment for all of our available man-power, in peace as well as in war time." In "Economic Preparedness for Defence and Post-Defence Problems," Federal Reserve Bulletin (January 1941), p. 12.

use its extraordinary wartime powers to regulate and commandeer economic life depends largely on the degree of voluntary co-operation offered by the several economic factors and by the general public, and on their knowledge and willingness to subordinate private aims to national necessities. The people can, with discipline and determination, carry through many measures which must otherwise be imposed by the state.

In total war the entire population is involved, and economic mobilization is a very important element in military strategy.

ORGANIZATION OF WAR ECONOMY

The experiences of the last war, analysed and discussed in many excellent books and by the governments themselves, have served as a guiding rule for the organization of war economy, so that the second world war has found every country far better prepared than before in economic strategy. The most comprehensive and detailed plan was, of course, prepared and put into operation by Germany.

The main task of any war economy consists in organizing production and labour to provide the maximum supply of goods and services and in adjusting civilian consumption to war necessities and priorities on a large scale. But at the same time attempts have been made to avoid some of the mistakes and failures of the last war: inflation, war profiteering, and great social changes; and care has been taken to prevent the profound dislocations in production which lead to undesirable post-war repercussions.

The scope of the general plan and the various special tasks of the war economy have been the principal determinants of the extent of state interference and commandeering of economic factors. Of prime importance is the general planning of the war economy in its most vital phases. Such planning must involve at present the organization of practically all parts of economic life. I shall consider here only certain of the more important elements and general problems, and then turn to the development and organization of the German and British war economies.

War Financing

The magnitude of expenditures attendant upon the organization of war economies has changed the character of war financing, but has also increased our knowledge. Money has become an instrument of financing, a transportation medium; no country will permit itself to lose a war because of financial difficulties. One comes to think in terms of real economy with primary emphasis on securing the necessary supply of goods and services —once this is assured, the necessary financial mechanism is to be provided. Of course this mechanism must be organized in such a way as to facilitate the satisfying of war needs and to avoid disturbances. The volume of a war budget is a clear indication of the position of the state; the state which previous to this war was absorbing —especially in Europe—a strikingly greater part of national income must now influence in ever greater degree the whole economic life. Financial policy becomes integrated in the whole economic war strategy, views which are merely budgetary being too narrow and limited to be accommodated to the general task.

The first concern of the financial policy must be to obtain that part of the national income which is needed for the prosecution of the war, in a manner which disturbs economic life as little as possible. Consumption must be adjusted and the level of prices and incomes managed so as to avoid inflation and profiteering.

Financial policy thus merges with price and income policies and with control of the capital market, and all are related to the main task of meeting war expenses, and of achieving balances between production and consumption and between military and civilian consumption. No separate budget is possible, since all measures must be fully integrated in the general economic plan.

The experiences of the last war have led to the most serious attempts by all nations to avoid inflation, which for our purpose we understand as a rise in the level of prices, making no distinction between a rise in the level of prices due primarily to monetary causes (inflation[1] in the proper sense) and a rise due to causes relating to commodities and services. In other words, the state's expenditures must be covered by non-inflationary means. But the "pay as you go" principle cannot be applied to a great modern war. In a non-monetary economy all necessary provision can be effected by direct requisition but in a capitalistic economy the people cannot be psychologically prepared to support the entire burden by taxes. The normal method of financing includes loans as well as taxes. The problem itself is clear: the state requires a part of the national income for war. How does this affect the remaining part, which constitutes the level of living? Ideally the state's requirements would be met by an actual increase in income. If, for instance, the national income rose from 100 to 140 to cover a new state requirement of 40, the nation's real income would remain unchanged in spite of the additional work and the increased volume of goods and services.

Unfortunately this cannot be expected in total war. Enormous state demands curtail the real income remaining for civilian consumption, no matter how wealthy the

---

[1] In my book *Theory of Inflation* published in 1922 by Komensky's University, Bratislava, I defined inflation as the spending of newly created purchasing power without adequate supply of new commodities.

economy may be.[1] The following situation then develops. An income increase from 100 to 140 is normally attended by a state demand of not 40 but 60, which leaves for civilian consumption only 80—20 per cent less than before the war. In other words, if the market situation is to remain unchanged—if inflation is not to develop—it is necessary to divert also this 20 per cent from the consuming public to the government. The danger of inflation is averted only by transferring to the state the purchasing power which usually is employed for consumption; the level of living is depressed. If, on the other hand, the state does not succeed in obtaining this 20 per cent of purchasing power but is instead obliged to extend the volume of credit, then the total market demand for goods is greater than the total of goods being offered (the total real income), and the state of inflation has been reached. Keynes, speaking of this inflationary " gap ", measures it by the difference between earnings available for expenditure and the value of the consumers' goods available for purchase at present prices.[2]

It is generally considered legitimate and even stimulating to extend credit in cyclical periods of unemployment and idle productive capacity, but the intensity of war demands the exercise of great caution in using this method of financing; the war economy cannot be regulated according to the normal principles of business cycles policy.

As already stated, the real burden of war cannot be shifted to the future. And the state must excise the necessary purchasing power in the form of taxes and of loans subscribed out of real savings. Only the acquisition

[1] R. M. Hettlage, *Deutscher Volkswirt* (December 20, 1940), p. 475: The increased need can never be provided for merely by an increased production if civilian consumption remains unchanged.

[2] *Financial News* (London, March 10, 1941), p. 2.

of some form of real income from foreign countries makes possible the shifting of the burden from nation to nation and thus from generation to generation.

There are many theories regarding the form of taxes best suited to war financing. Such views comprise much that calls for respect, although war demands are so great and so urgent that it becomes extremely difficult to follow consistently any theoretical line. Income and corporation taxes, collected at the source if possible, are regarded as most appropriate, since they cut down purchasing power and tend to reduce war profits. On the other hand, it is rightly pointed out that very high excess-profit taxes decrease incentive for greater production and furthermore tend to raise costs of production through removing the pressure to economize.

The volume of expenditures, however, cannot be met by income taxes alone; even taxes on consumers' goods may have to be applied. The latter device may support the measures curtailing civilian consumption, but they are likely to raise prices at the same time. The main argument against such taxes is often that they discourage civilian consumption and thus reduce employment. The criticism is valid for a period of depression. But it cannot be maintained when the state's leading purpose is precisely to curtail consumption.

In any case, a considerable proportion of the expenditures will have to be covered by loans. From the point of view of avoiding inflation, these loans should have the same economic effect as taxes, i.e. they should transfer to the state purchasing power which otherwise would have been devoted to consumption. The demand is that the loans be paid out of real savings, thus effecting a voluntary renunciation of consumption. The term " saving " here acquires an unusual connotation, since its use is not for productive but in fact for destructive purposes. Loans to the state by banks or private subscribers which are financed through an extension of bank credit cannot in this respect be considered real savings. Even the use of funds which before their transfer to the state were held idle in banks has not the same character as a transfer of real savings.

It is an important and difficult task to organize additional saving and thus to divert to the state the necessary purchasing power. There are various devices which may be employed to support savings campaigns, but much depends on the people's determination, patriotism, and confidence in the state's financial stability. Although rates of interest, like the prices of goods, are under state control, manipulation of these rates is not very effective as an instrument for increasing saving. For while the state may thereby exercise persuasion and even pressure on big corporations, banks, and insurance companies, still the full amount of needed credit cannot be supplied by these means. Other methods of promoting savings and subscription to state loans work on the side of goods as well as on the side of capital. Rationing and priority adjustments in investment and also in civilian consumption constitute such procedures. Obviously foreign exchange control is established to conserve national capital. Licensing of public emissions reserves the market for state loans; controlling the credit policy of banks serves the same purpose. Also various proposals of compulsory savings have been made, among them the well-known deferred payment plan proposed by Keynes. Some forms of concealed compulsory saving may become necessary in case the public fails to reduce its expenditures voluntarily.[1]

[1] The German Minister of National Economy, Walther Funk, writes: "Compulsion and severity in proposals for concentrated war savings can be avoided if everyone acts voluntarily to conform to wartime needs. An exaggerated consumption must be subjected to additional taxation." *Deutscher Volkswirt*, January 5, 1940.

There are various reasons for preferring taxation to loans. One is that the effect of loans on consumption is never as great as that of taxes. Pigou points out that, although in loan financing rich people bear a somewhat larger proportion of the war charges than they do of normal peace charges, under the tax method their contribution is even more substantial.[1] This may indeed need modification in the light of post-war debts and post-war settlements, and with regard to the immediate policy of reducing war profits. There is a definite tendency in the economics of total war to impose on everyone sacrifices from which there is and will be no escape.

But as the state's expenditures grow and as war needs require an ever greater part of the national income, the task of collecting the necessary funds without inflation[2] becomes more and more difficult. The problem is that of distinguishing between the part of national income required by the state and that remaining for civilian consumption, and of transferring the required purchasing power without causing a greater rise in the price level. Judging by the German experience, this should always be possible. We read : " The free purchasing power when collected will in the end flow completely to the state. This free purchasing power is necessarily approximately adequate to the state's credit need, which can never be greater than the total amount of goods and services demanded by the state. No difficulties of financing can arise."[3]

---

[1] Pigou, *The Political Economy of War*, p. 83.

[2] The effects of inflation in increasing production are overestimated, and the complications and dangers of the process are somewhat disregarded by those who advocate a moderate inflation. For instance, Douglas Jay says, "A little moderate and planned inflation may not do such very terrible harm." *Who Is to Pay for the War* (Kegan Paul, Trench, Trübner, London, 1941), p. 15.

[3] R. M. Hettlage, *Deutscher Volkswirt* (December 20, 1940), pp. 475-80.

But if the war demands such a large part of national income that, despite all organization and mechanical devices, popular resistance appears likely, then the state will certainly not hesitate to have recourse to an inflationary credit expansion. And some inflationary effects will develop in spite of all possible controls and regimentation. The point at which inflation will become necessary depends upon the real income, morale, the duration of the war, and the organization of the war economy. It is not identical with the point of exhaustion of the real economy, which is located where the war need can no longer be satisfied by further reductions in civilian consumption or by forcing further production, and where the prosecution of the war is actually menaced by the insufficiency of the real war fund. Of course this point, too, is reached more quickly if the war organization, including the financial mechanism, does not function efficiently.

Control of Prices and Incomes

The problem of avoiding inflation—increased price and income levels—cannot be solved in wartime by financial and monetary policy alone, since there is a danger that inflationary effects may be brought about by non-monetary causes. The sudden demand for armament at the beginning of the war, and, following it or simultaneous with it, the general increase in demand for all kinds of goods and services must influence the market, prices, and wages. Bottlenecks appear first in armament and related industries, but the increased volume of income spreads demand very rapidly through the whole market, buying tendency grows, and the danger of price increases becomes acute, passing finally from fully employed segments to other segments of the economy. Two forces operate to change the pattern of demand:

war needs of all kinds, and the generally increased income of the working classes, whose consumption develops in certain definite directions. Very illuminating here are figures regarding the distribution of British national income among the main income groups in 1940. The share of wages in the total national income increased from 41 per cent in 1938 to 44½ per cent in 1940 (45 per cent in the last quarter of 1940), whereas rents declined from 8 per cent to 6½ per cent and salaries from 22 per cent to 20½ per cent.[1] Such a change in the distribution of national income must affect directly the market for consumption goods.

The best way to meet increased demand in these two large sectors of national economy would, of course, be the expanding of national production and thus the attaining of a new equilibrium, as is generally the case during business cycles. But this will not be possible during wartime even in the wealthiest economy, and as the war progresses it becomes more and more difficult. There may be some exceptions in industrially undeveloped countries having large natural resources and the ability to use modern manufacturing technique and equipment. War needs increase and labour resources decline. Moreover, it is always difficult to determine how far to extend production and productive capacity in the new armament sectors : it is not easy to make an accurate estimate of the volume of war needs and the extent to which they will require the transformation of civilian production to war industry ; again, the experiences of the last war discourage such expansion in view of the post-war difficulties of once more transforming production and returning labour from war to peace work.[2] This does

[1] *Economist* (1941), p. 489.
[2] Marriner S. Eccles, Federal Reserve Bulletin (January 1941), p. 13: "A price inflation, due to non-monetary causes, arises when production in particular fields is interrupted or curtailed, whether from bottlenecks,

War Economy 49

not mean that increased production is not the best way to meet the threat of rising prices.

A certain increase of prices (and, as we have seen, a certain extension of the volume of credit) may, in the early stages of the war, be useful and perhaps necessary to stimulate the national economy to the optimum of production.[1] But the expansion of production caused by the rise in prices and wages which follows from the volume of war demand is substantially limited, and the danger of the well-known vicious spiral of prices-wages-prices is extremely great. Price increases from particular bottlenecks have a tendency to spread to the general price level, and, as John H. Williams rightly says, "Under modern conditions there is no clean cut line between what we call bottleneck problems and a general inflation."[2]

We have already pointed out that under conditions of war the law of supply and demand is suspended; the state has a predominant position in the markets and can determine prices and incomes. If the anti-inflationary financial and monetary policy is to be effective in preventing a rise in the level of prices from non-monetary causes, the state must establish, over and above measures for increasing production, a definite national policy affecting

---

short-sighted wage and price policies, monopolistic practices by capital or labour, or related causes, when there is pressing consumer demand for the goods produced in these fields and when there is neither a shortage of facilities that exist or can be constructed, nor a shortage of man power. The cure for such a condition is not less but more production." It seems to me that the conclusion of Mr Eccles is too optimistic to be valid in a war economy.

[1] But " beyond the early stage when the total volume of productive effort is still increasing, any further increase in the money stream does nothing to promote the mobilization programme, and its indirect consequences are adverse." Charles O. Hardy, *Wartime Control of Prices* (Brookings Institute, 1940), p. 10.

[2] Federal Reserve Bulletin (February 1941), p. 97.

prices and wages. These, of course, should be closely interrelated parts of a single economic programme.

Control or even regimentation of prices and wages cannot succeed if the monetary and financial policy follows an inflationary course ; and, on the other hand, anti-inflationary monetary and financial measures cannot be fully efficient if prices and wages are permitted to go up in consequence of the situations created by bottlenecks and other factors.

The whole financial policy must be flexible enough to adjust itself to particular needs, to avoid the discouragement of production, and to stimulate special efforts and initiative. And the policy must be comprehensive, since it is impossible to freeze prices in one economic sector if those in another important sector are permitted to rise, or to freeze wages if prices go up, and vice versa. An effective price strategy will involve stabilizing and controlling the most important components of costs of production and the prices of key commodities. This may be done in many ways.

The vital importance of stability in wages and other incomes is evident. In democratic countries it will be found difficult to use compulsion in wage policy, and the procedures of persuasion and mediation will be preferred. Perhaps the British system of linking wages with the cost of living index, in spite of some serious defects, may prove most appropriate for the war economy. As stated, wages cannot remain stable if the cost of living tends to rise. In the control and regulation of prices the government has an efficient weapon : as the greatest single buyer it can influence the price level when placing government orders. Price controls, if they are to succeed, must be introduced in time and at the source.

Where a system of maximum prices is applied to commodities of which there is an adequate supply it is often found that prices are stabilized at a level below the maximum. On the other hand, if maximum prices are set for commodities of insufficient supply, it is necessary to complement this programme with a rationing of consumers' goods or with a system of priorities in industrial production. Rationing has been steadily extended in Germany, based not only upon quantity of goods but also upon the amount to be spent at any given time. In England it has even been proposed to limit individual retail expenditures, as the most efficient expedient for regulating the distribution of goods and curtailing purchasing power.[1] Another device consists in state purchases or imports, with the state acting as sole buyer, importer, or even distributor. And again, a useful and important instrument of an active price policy may be some kind of an equalization fund for subsidizing important consumers' goods and thus keeping the whole price level down. The general expenses incurred in such subsidizing are to be preferred to price increases in vital commodities, since the effects of the collection and spending of these amounts are felt far less than are rising prices.

National price and wage policy should attempt in every possible way to maintain the pre-war relations among prices of various commodities and among individual components of the cost of production (including groups of incomes). This will at once facilitate the operation of the general price programme and prevent unnecessary dislocations which may impede post-war reconstruction.

All price and wage controls and administration belong to the most complicated phase of economic organization for war. And they are far more difficult to handle in democracies than in totalitarian states which can employ all possible methods of thorough supervision

[1] *Financial News* (London, April 3, 1941), p. 2.

and compulsion.[1] Democracies, relying on co-operation, discipline, and the willingness of labour and capital to make sacrifices, will always be slower to start. They must persuade rather than compel. But they must prove that they are able to achieve by democratic methods the necessary economic results: development of war production, adjustment of consumption to war necessities, and immunity of the social structure to the impact of war.

Mobilization of Production and Labour

Mobilization of the nation's production—of industry, agriculture, and labour—is the second part of the same supreme task: that of organizing the war economy to satisfy all needs arising from the prosecution of the war. The first concern is to increase work and production; but it is over simple to approach the problem by balancing the total demand against the total labour and productive capacity plus the total volume of national production and income. A similar fallacy is involved in taking together idle plants, idle capacity, and unemployed labour and attempting thereby to measure the general possibility of satisfying the increased war demands. (Such reasoning might lead to the false conclusion that national productive capacity if fully employed would be large enough to satisfy both civilian and war demands.) To assume that, by the use of all dispensable capacity and the employment of all labour, the balance between supply and demand may be maintained is to anticipate that the vertical

---

[1] In the Russian economy, which is in its basic structure similar to a natural (real) economy, the solution of this whole problem should be much more simple. Even as Russia curtailed mass civilian consumption by rationing the total expenditure on consumers' goods in order to build up heavy industry, so she can in wartime, by using similar direct methods, divert the required part of production and income. Such an economy need not have recourse to the indirect controls of prices, taxes, etc. The severe control in the German war economy has approached the Russian both in conception and in organization.

structure of production will conform to the vertical structure of demand as increased and changed by the new needs. We have already seen that demand is not only increased but also changed in its vertical structure; these modifications follow from war requirements and from the structural alterations in civilian demand consequent upon the increased income of labour. Totalitarian economies in preparing for war have the advantage of an easier adjustment of production to war demands. In democratic countries the shift from peace to war production is very difficult for technical, economic, and psychological reasons. People are slow to recognize the need for adjusting production and confining it to war necessities, and slow—unless danger is realized—to prepare to work more and consume less.

From an analysis of the relation between the structure of production and skilled labour and the composition of demand, or from an examination of the conditions of the new quantitative and qualitative balance between limited supply and practically unlimited demand, it should not be very difficult to determine how far it is advisable to expand credit and increase prices. Although the answer may vary according to the structure and amplitude of the resources of various national economies, the problem of adjustment remains everywhere in developed national economies substantially the same.

It is very important to assure in this field the most complete co-operation of industry and labour, because in spite of the limited place left for the profit motive in every war economy, this is the kind of activity in which private initiative and imagination can be extremely helpful. The fiscal policy must be careful, therefore, not to create an atmosphere hostile to private initiative.

Notwithstanding the increase in production and employment, national production in the belligerent countries is no longer able to satisfy the whole demand. In totalitarian economies, the state achieves the adjustment of consumption by a combination of commandeered industry and comprehensive rationing. Lack of adequate production may be due partly to technical or labour bottlenecks in single segments of industry. Such bottlenecks can be overcome, if time and physical possibilities permit, by expansion of existing industry and the building of new plants, and by the training of new skilled labour. In a full war economy, however, because of the complicated interrelations of highly developed industries, bottlenecks tend to multiply quickly, and state interference to regulate supply becomes urgent. The method most often used for this purpose is the system of priorities (production of goods for war before all other commodities), which may be imposed directly or by indirect means, such as rationing of the supply of labour or raw materials, transport control, and so forth. The conception of priorities is clearly inherent in that of a war economy, where the general demand is that everything be subordinated to war purposes. This should be kept in mind in defining the system of priorities.[1]

The important position of the priorities system in the organization of war economy is described in the following extremely pertinent statement by Bernard M. Baruch : " Any industrial mobilization must have as the centre of everything a priorities division which synchronizes the whole war effort, at the same time providing for the maximum satisfaction of civilian needs. To be efficient, the priorities administration must also

---

[1] John H. Martin defines the system of priorities as " a method of guiding industrial equipment and services into uses which will serve most effectively the total national defence," " Present Status of Priorities;" *Harvard Business Review* (Spring 1941), p. 272.

Pigou says that priorities regulate distribution among uses rather than among people. *The Political Economy of War*, p. 157.

envisage price and money control, conservation, inventions, commandeering, and the use of substitutes. Lastly, but no less important, priorities and price control will ensure that the nation not only wins the war but *survives* it economically, with a low price structure and an industrial system dislocated to a minimum degree, well prepared for post-war conditions in the international markets."[1]

This statement also emphasizes the importance of organizing a comprehensive national war economy, in which one part is closely linked with another to form a definite general plan. By implication it points to that stage of development which in the present war has already been reached by both Germany and Great Britain. All productive equipment, all industry, is to be treated as if it were one big enterprise governed from one place and by one set of principles. These war economies are in the stage of fully mobilized production and labour. Scarcity of labour, in addition to other factors, forces them to curtail much of normal peacetime production. The problem is to rationalize this production sector thoroughly in order to free more labour for war industry. Production previously carried on in several partially employed plants is centralized in one or more fully occupied "nucleus" factories; surplus labour is directed into war production. The employment of labour in trade and similar occupations is equally rationalized, and the work of women is extended. Thus both industry and labour are practically conscripted; both have to surrender some of their rights. Labour is asked to work longer hours, and capital to close factories temporarily and merge production in a common plant. The need for labour has been greater than was anticipated. There is

[1] Baruch, "Priorities, the Synchronizing Force," *Harvard Business Review* (Spring 1941), p. 270.

the urgent problem of maintaining and even increasing agricultural production, in which labour is the most important factor. And it has been estimated that to produce the equipment and other supplies required by one soldier, from ten to eighteen workers are needed.

Democracies obviously prefer to achieve mobilization of labour and industry not by compulsion but by co-operation, resting on the patriotic determination of the people. The actual progress of the war has revealed the growing importance of the working army to the fighting forces ; the war goes on in genuinely total fashion. It goes without saying that in this stage of war it becomes more and more difficult to make the replacements necessary for keeping factories in desirable condition—a part of the national substance is inevitably lost. And it is equally obvious that when the total social product declines under the pressure of war production, income and certainly consumption tend to contract. Nor is it any contradiction to the economy of total war that a general increase in labour duty is accompanied by heavier taxation and compulsory saving. The meaning of sacrifices is made amply clear.

It need hardly be said that foreign trade control is integrated in the whole production programme and subordinated to war purposes. Exports are regarded only as a device for securing the necessary commodity imports, and the proper rôle of foreign trade declines in importance.

In summary, the task and objective—whether on the side of production or on the side of financing the war—are the same : to satisfy the practically unlimited demands originating in the war as far as possible through greater national production, but in the end also by curtailing existing civilian consumption. War demands have priority; other needs have to give way. The problem is that of organizing the productive and financial capacities of the nation as efficiently and rapidly as possible, and with the least possible social disturbance. Never before have the democracies faced a task of such proportions, importance, and danger.

CHAPTER III

THE WAR ECONOMIES OF GERMANY AND GREAT BRITAIN

GERMANY

At the beginning of the war Germany enjoyed a great advantage over the other countries for two reasons. First, she possessed a huge store of armament, of raw materials, and even of food. Second, her industrial capacity and her economy generally had been highly organized along the lines of pre-war defence economy. As the German Reichsbank stated, in its annual report for 1939, " The transition to wartime activity, thanks to the work of organization accomplished in the preceding years, has been rapidly and smoothly completed, enabling the economy to achieve the expansion of its productive capacity necessary to meet the wartime needs."[1] Germany began the war with a comprehensive and totalitarian controlled economic organization which was readily extended to meet all the important new tasks imposed by the war emergency.

The general war strategy was formulated principally with a short war in view—a *Blitzkrieg*. But from the beginning, some measures were taken to cover a longer period (such as comprehensive rationing[2] of consumption

---

[1] Federal Reserve Bulletin (September 1940), p. 942.
According to a German official, State Secretary Körner, " We are far ahead of our enemies, whose economic organization remains still extremely hesitant and incomplete." From *Vierjahresplan* (January 5, 1940), as quoted by H. W. Singer in " The German War Effort in the Light of Economic Periodicals," *Economic Journal* (1941), pp. 19-35.

[2] A member of the German High Command, Becker, asserted that " Rationing of vitally important consumption was only an organic continuation of the peace economy." *Deutscher Volkswirt* (1941), p. 29.

at a time when this was not needed to maintain supplies). As we shall see later, the economic phase of the general strategy was not without influence on military policy.

The purpose in the actual war is the same as that of any other country—to increase production for war as much as possible and to mobilize all economic resources even more completely than under the defence economy. The general methods were: complete conscription of labour, extended rationing of civilian consumption and curtailing of non-defence production, centralized commandeering and gearing of production by allocation of raw materials and labour, stabilization of the general price and wage level, and control of foreign trade and foreign exchange. Consumption was curtailed as far as possible in order to make any recourse to inflationary methods unnecessary. In other words, the state sought through a wholesale economic regimentation to achieve the maximum efficiency indispensable to the conduct of the war.

Although it is difficult to obtain official figures on many sectors of the German economy—various statistics were suppressed before the war started and others later—we shall try to determine how far this war effort was successful.

Price control, linked with rationing of consumption, is the most important item in the general policy and especially in war financing in Germany: it continues and perfects the programme initiated in the price-stop order issued on November 26, 1936. This order prohibited all increases in prices and wages from the level of October 16, 1936. The wholesale price index on that date was 104·3 (where the 1913 level is taken as 100), the total cost of living index 124·4, and the wage-rate index 83·6.

Price and wage control was systematically developed with a view to flexibility in meeting various necessities in production and to elimination of war profits. The cost of production was subjected to various types of supervision.[1] At the beginning of the war the original price-stop order was modified to effect a complex system of cost prices on the one hand and drastic measures to keep down final prices and wages on the other. The decree of September 4, 1939, aimed at lowering the cost of public orders—in view of the high profits in mechanized production—without change in wages or in the prices of consumers' goods. In December, 1940, a number of new price orders were issued, establishing *inter alia* a new system of determining prices, after the Supreme Court had declared in November of that year that the price-stop decree was still in force.[2] Revenue so secured from excess profits was to be employed by the Treasury to lower the prices of various important commodities, such as those filling public orders, though not of consumers' goods. And the tax was to be sufficiently flexible to facilitate production in new plants or in emergency plants where costs of production were high.

Official indices point to success so far in maintenance of price and wage stability. The cost of living rose from 127 in August 1939 to 132 in April 1941, or only 3·9 per cent; wholesale prices from 107·1 to 112, or only 4·5 per cent, in the same period; and retail food prices from 122 in September 1939 to 126 in March 1941, or only 3·3 per cent. These figures are, however, misleading in that they do not reveal deterioration in quality or the unavailability of certain articles of consumption.[3]

Wages have been supervised as closely as prices. When the war began, all extra pay for overtime was prohibited.

[1] *Economist* (1941), p. 341.
[2] *Ibid.*
[3] *The Danger of Inflation in the United States and Wartime Price Control in Germany and Great Britain* (Institute of International Finance, New York University, Bulletin No. 114, March 17, 1941), p. 14.

After some months it was again permitted, but only for hours of work exceeding ten a day, the extra pay for the ninth and tenth hours being turned over to the Treasury. Specially high wages were permitted for labour in new or very important industries, etc. But the War Wage Order early in the war ended the differentiation of wage levels which had been effected through special classifications of workers according to skill, special bonuses, and other devices.[1]

Germany's defence economy had achieved practically complete mobilization before the war. The change to wartime production was therefore less radical than in other countries, but still involved a drastic increase in the regimentation of labour and industry. This had begun in direct form on June 21, 1938, following the Czechoslovakian political crisis of a month before, when a decree was issued empowering the Central Labour Exchange to "mobilize all German citizens, men and women, to do for a limited period the work allocated to them in the interest of the Reich".

At the outbreak of the war this required labour took the form of a military mobilization, and workers and employers became subject to special training for war work. Compulsory labour has now widened to supply a substantial portion of the increase in production as the shift from peacetime to armament production has gone forward.[2] Many thousands had to be specially trained for war production, and the German Labour Front supplied 16,000 instructors to train them.[3] Commissioners examine the factories to ensure the best use of skilled labour, and all changes in employment are subject to

[1] *Deutscher Volkswirt* (March 15, 1941).

[2] By the end of 1940, 1,750,000 workers had been gradually called up for compulsory labour.

[3] *Economist* (November 23, 1940), p. 641.

ruling by the labour exchange. The worker, like the soldier, is tied to his job. Although the principle of maximum hours remains officially in force, the working day may be arbitrarily increased to ten hours for men and the working week to fifty-six hours for women and minors. Compulsory labour for those under military age has been extended to all single women and to childless married women between eighteen and fifty.

Despite all these measures, skilled labour is considered a greater bottleneck in the German economy than the supply of raw materials.[1] Every effort has been made to economize on labour in the non-armament industries as well as in the trades and professions. Labour has been imported from occupied countries and from Italy; agriculture has absorbed more than one and a half million prisoners and civilian foreign workers. And industrial workers are being drawn from all the Continent into the vacuum created by the intensified draft of soldiers in Germany.

The following orders issued on June 15, 1940, by the German Ministry of Labour indicate the intensity of the mobilization of labour: calling up all reserves through closing down unnecessary plants; combing out of industry all non-essential jobs; larger employment of women; steering all unattached labour into the points of greatest urgency; and a most searching examination of all demand. It is evident that after the intensive pre-war production a new increase could be achieved only by a complete mobilization of resources and labour and a longer working day. The entire industrial production was commandeered as a unit by the state so as to concentrate output in the most efficient plants. It was the task of the General Council for War Economy to unify the whole of the policy by co-ordinating the executive

[1] Cf. New York *Times*, April 28, 1941, p. 23, and July 24, 1941, p. 4.

functions of the various departments of the central administration and of the regional administrations. Although free initiative was extremely limited, the authorities have attempted to develop co-operation with private industry and to maintain a certain flexibility in the whole system.[1]

We have no exact knowledge of the German national income for this period and must rely on inferences from certain official or semi-official statements. It was estimated to be in 1938 about 79,700,000,000 reichsmarks —including Austria and the Sudetan part of Czechoslovakia, about 87-88,000,000,000 reichsmarks.[2] Dr. Reinhardt, State Secretary of Finance, estimated the national income of Greater Germany for 1940-41 at 100,000,000,000 reichsmarks.[3] (We do not know exactly how much of Poland and other conquered territories this term covers.)[4] This would mean an increase in national income, production, and services maximum of about 13 per cent for the first year of the war. But it is doubtful whether this rise could continue, in view of the completeness of industrial mobilization, without resources from abroad. In any case, during this year the increase fell far short of the new demands. Some illustration may be found in the total receipts from sales of agricultural products for Germany proper, including supplies for the military forces; these increased from 10,694,000,000 in 1938-39 to 10,948,000,000 reichsmarks in 1939-40, in other

[1] For this effort to unite central control with local initiative and individual enterprise, see *Economist* (May 17, 1941), p. 660.

[2] The *Frankfurter Zeitung*, quoted by De Wilde, in *Foreign Policy Reports* for July 15, 1940.

[3] The official rate for the reichsmark is quoted nominally at about 2s.

[4] Karl M. Hettlage, " Who Pays for the War ? ", *Deutscher Volkswirt* (December 20, 1940), p. 475, estimates German national production in 1940 at 85,000,000,000 reichsmarks.

words, by only 2·4 per cent. (The figure in 1937-38 was 9,976,000,000 reichsmarks.)[1]

The fear of inflation resulting from the experience of the first World War and of the post-war period made Germany particularly anxious to avoid its recurrence. To this end the various measures of control were carried out in close connection with an intended non-inflationary system of war financing.

The publication of the regular budget was discontinued in 1934. On the basis of official statements and inference, we may suppose that Germany was able to meet nearly half her expenses by taxes and the rest by loans. Revenues from taxes and other sources increased steadily as a result of the rise in national income and the higher fiscal efficiency attendant on total control of the economy. The War Emergency Decree of September 4, 1939, imposed a 50 per cent surtax on incomes (the general income tax began on incomes of over 2,400 reichsmarks a year and on wages of over 54 reichsmarks a week) and a 20 per cent increase in beer and tobacco taxes. In addition, states and municipalities have been ordered to

[1] The detailed figures are:

AGRICULTURAL SALES (in millions of reichsmarks)

	1937-38	1938-39	1939-40
Cereals	1,644	2,267	2,015
Potatoes for human consumption	446	470	560
Potatoes—total	629	648	733
Sugar	702	574	619
Fruit	375	117	368
Vegetables	210	217	232
Total plant products	3,880	4,162	4,326
Total livestock for slaughter	3,556	3,722	3,577
Total dairy and animal products	6,056	6,532	6,622
Milk	2,025	2,302	2,465

These figures show that in Germany's wartime diet the consumption of meat and other high-quality foodstuffs has been reduced in favour of potatoes (which rose by 19 per cent) and vegetables and sugar (which rose by 8 per cent). Increases in receipts from milk and dairy products resulted from statutory increases in prices. See the *Economist* (June 7, 1941), p. 761.

increase their contributions to the central government.[1] As all profits were controlled at the source, an excess profits tax was considered unnecessary.

Revenues of the Reich increased from 6,800,000,000 reichsmarks in 1933 to 17,700,000,000 reichsmarks in 1938 and to 23,600,000,000 in 1939. For the fiscal year ending March 31, 1940, the tax receipts were estimated at 25,000,000,000, and for 1940-41 at the record figure of 27,200,000,000.[2] Reinhardt estimates the corresponding amount for 1941-42 at 30,000,000,000 reichsmarks; other normal revenues are expected to yield 5,000,000,000, and the contribution of the German local communities will provide 1,400,000,000 more. Finally, the annual payments (contributions or reparations) of the protectorates toward the German expenses in the seven occupied countries are calculated at 3,600,000,000. The total revenue should thus reach about 40,000,000,000 reichsmarks. Taxes and other ordinary revenues collected within Germany were absorbing about 35 per cent of the national income, put at 100,000,000,000 marks.[3] To this we must add the levies of provincial and local governments and various substantial contributions, which are voluntary in name only ("Winter Help," "People's Cars," etc.). The financial burden on the German people is very heavy and cannot be successfully increased in any considerable degree.

The 55 per cent of war expenditures not covered by

[1] J. R. Hicks, U. K. Hicks, and L. Rostas, *The Taxation of War Wealth* (Clarendon Press, Oxford, 1941), p. 147.

[2] New York *Times*, May 18, 1941.

During the first quarter of the current fiscal year, which ended on June 30, 1941, taxes, direct and indirect, and customs yielded 7,176,000,000 reichsmarks compared with 6,067,000,000 reichsmarks during the corresponding period of 1940. Statement by Reinhardt on August 2, 1941. New York *Times*, August 4, 1941, p. 6.

[3] Cf. also the appendix to the annual report of the Bank of Canada for 1940 containing Governor Towers's memorandum on German war finance.

taxes and other regular revenues had to be met by borrowing. For. the fiscal year 1940-41, the Reich's expenditures amounted to about 68,200,000,000 reichsmarks, whereas revenues from taxes and other sources came to only 30,200,000,000, so that its debt rose in the period by 38,000,000,000 reichsmarks.[1] The general economic organization made relatively easy the securing of this balance : as the Reichsbank said, " Restrictions upon the general standard of living through curtailing output of consumption goods has directed increasing attention to the importance, from the standpoint of currency policy, of skimming off and concentrating the surplus purchasing power of the German economy."[2] Germany did not openly employ any form of compulsory saving or forced loans, but the completeness of the economic control made this type of saving far from voluntary. Civilian spending is under an all-embracing ration system ;· industry may enter into new enterprise only by government permission and in conformity with allocations of raw materials ; trade cannot freely replenish depleted inventories. Thus the real savings of the population—the liquid capital resulting partly from not replenishing stocks, making replacements, or investing in new ventures, and partly from higher profits—have no outlet other than as deposits with banks and credit institutions, in buying of government securities, or in buying of common stocks.

[1] New York *Times*, June 8, 1941. *Statist* for April 26, 1941, on p. 364, gives the following figures : official expenditures for the 18 months from July 1939, to December 1940, were 83,243,000,000 reichsmarks, or nearly the total of 86,875,000,000 for the six years from April 1933, to March 1939. In 1938-39 these expenditures stood at 29,288,000,000, in 1939-40 at 47,963,000,000, and in 1940-41 at about 64,000,000,000 (although other official sources estimate them at 68,200,000,000). In the calendar year 1940 borrowing is estimated at 33,124,000,000, or 56 per cent of apparent expenditures; other receipts reached only 26,250,000,000, or only 44 per cent.

[2] Federal Reserve Bulletin (September 1940), pp. 942-3.

The only real outlet for buying non-rationed commodities is the stock exchange, which consequently registered a rise in the market values of common stocks from 93·2 in August 1939, to 115·9 in August 1940, and to 131·1 in April 1941, in spite of the limitation of dividends to 6 per cent of their face value and repeated official warnings.[1] The sharp upward movement continued with the stock price index steadily going up in June and July. This movement of common stock prices in Germany together with a similar tendency in the occupied countries (for instance common stock prices on the Prague Stock Exchange) can be taken as an indication of the definite existence of the inflationary fear and nervousness. Therefore a practice has been introduced of limiting daily increases in quotations of individual shares to 1 or 1½ per cent of their value. Proposals of introducing a market organization as it exists for virtually all German commodity markets or the fixing of security prices are surprisingly regarded as impracticable since such measures would destroy the vital function of the stock exchange. Strenuous efforts are, of course, made to increase the saving of and subscription to government bonds, and some fiscal measures were adopted for that purpose. (There is also the permanent "advice" to companies with great liquid funds to invest them in government securities.) The German people prefer savings in the form of bank deposits to securities, and as the war has progressed, the total of such savings has risen rapidly. (The total wartime savings up to the end of 1940 were 8,000,000,000 reichsmarks, bringing the total of savings deposits to 30,000,000,000 reichsmarks.[2] And

[1] Federal Reserve Bulletin, July, 1941, p. 717. New York *Times*, July 18, 1941, p. 21.
[2] New York *Times*, March 13, 1941, p. 2.
Dr Ernst Nölting in *Der Deutsche Volkswirt* (January 3, 1941), p. 557 : In the period August 31, 1939-August 31, 1940, the bank deposits increased

the only investment opening for the banks is government bonds. In fact, however, these accumulated savings deposits represent an immense purchasing power "blocked" without use, which constitutes a latent inflation that may suddenly come into the open unless checked by new restrictions. This is a serious weakness in the German "non-inflationary" financing.

Clearly in a capital market so administered it was not difficult to establish a cheap money policy. The percentage yield of government bonds sank from an average of 4·58 per cent in 1939 to 4·45 per cent in November, 1940,[1] and the index of bonds increased from 98·9 in September, 1939, to 101·4 in December 1940, and to 103 in April 1941. The rate on treasury bonds dropped from 4·5 per cent to 4 per cent and then to 3·5 per cent at the beginning of 1941, and the bank rate was reduced from 4 per cent to 3·5 per cent.[2] According to the Reichsbank's official statement, circulation of its notes developed as follows: July 31, 1939—8,980,000,000; August 31—10,900,000,000; December 30—11,790,000,000; December 31, 1940—14,030,000,000; April 30, 1941—14,680,000,000; and July 31, 1941—16,030,000,000. Although this increase is considerable, it cannot in itself be taken as proof of inflation. The Reichsbank explains the increase in the first year by the army's demand for large cash payments and reserves and by the expansion of the German economy attendant on the accession of territory (in which the rate of circulation was especially low).[3] Moreover it is argued that this increase

---

by more than 50 per cent and in the first six months of 1940 the deposits excess in savings banks was twice as big during the whole year 1939; that is, the total deposits was enlarged by one-third in one year.

[1] League of Nations, *Monthly Bulletin of Statistics* (March 1941), p. 84.
[2] *Economist* (March 22, 1941), p. 378.
[3] Federal Reserve Bulletin (September 1940), p. 944.

constitutes a very small proportion of the total war expenditure of the government. But the fact remains that the total currency circulation of 18,600,000,000 reichsmarks at the end of July (including the Reichsbanks' note circulation of 16,030,000,000, about 1,600,000,000 in coins, and 1,000,000,000 in Renten bank notes) represents an expansion of more then 70 per cent since the beginning of the war. This expansion, which was followed by a drastic contraction in the quantity of available consumer goods and which is increasing in larger proportion since the beginning of the war against Russia, has to be observed as one of the very important symptoms of the general situation. An expansion of currency circulation continues also in all countries occupied and controlled by Germany and Italy.

There is official opinion in Germany that this procedure of diverting surplus purchasing power to the state can continue indefinitely and that financing difficulties cannot arise. For, these officials contend, if an increase in physical requirements or in prices augments the war needs, larger funds will automatically become available to the state. They dismiss as irrelevant subordinate questions such as those connected with the level of interest rates.[1] But these arguments fail to recognize the limit in the ratio between the total purchasing power transferred to the state and the total national income. Whether—this I considered in Chapter II—the limit is to be set at 50 per cent or 55 per cent or 60 per cent depends on various factors, primary among which are the purchasing power represented by the remainder and the probable duration of the emergency.

The Reich's indebtedness was stated as of March 31, 1941, to be 90,000,000,000 reichsmarks, but it increased during the first quarter of 1941 at the rate of

[1] Hettlage, *Deutscher Volkswirt* (1940), p. 475.

3,500,000,000 a month (altogether 10,600,000,000) and the war against Russia will undoubtedly raise the current deficit to a considerable degree, making the financing problem very difficult. In the preceding sixteen months of the war, the monthly increase had been only 2,600,000,000.[1] In terms of the expected national income of 100,000,000,000 reichsmarks for the current year, this means that the state will consume about two-thirds of the national income, with a further increase in prospect. There would be reason to think that Germany has nearly reached the limit of this type of financing as well as of the general power of the economy to maintain itself. Here, however, definite reservations must be made.

Not all loans came from actual savings; a certain number must have been in the form of bank advances, and this will increase in the future. Others reflect diminished stocks or disinvestment—in other words, a reduction of capital; these were very considerable in the first year of the war, but their importance is now declining.[2] In the years to come there will be no such physical reserves in Germany, and the whole problem will be far more serious unless the reserves can be replaced by conquest and exploitation of foreign countries.

As I shall explain later, during the war Germany has further developed the system of clearing and barter agreements to acquire various necessary commodities on her own terms. Her resources have also been strengthened by large stocks of all kinds of commodities from conquered countries and by financial contributions from those

[1] New York *Times*, May 18, 1941.

[2] Hettlage estimates the capital consumed in 1940 at some 12,000,000,000 reichsmarks, of which 3-4,000,000,000 represents neglected replacements resulting from the use of stocks for war purposes, 5-6,000,000,000 the exhaustion of stocks of raw materials and goods, and the rest, decreased private formation of physical assets. He estimates the reduction of private consumption at 14,000,000,000 reichsmarks.

countries, estimated by R. A. Butler, British Under-Secretary for Foreign Affairs, at £1,150,000,000 a year, this including the French occupation payment.[1] More important is the fact that Germany organizes the economies of all the conquered countries to conform to her own needs. The financial and economic limits upon her capacity to carry on the war have been thus extended from her own economy to the economic organization and resources of nearly the entire European continent.

GREAT BRITAIN

When the war started there was a fundamental difference between the British and German economies and between the British and German conceptions of warfare. Great Britain's was a welfare economy governed according to democratic political principles and resting as a whole on freedom of enterprise. This economy had neither the techniques nor the basic preparation for a comprehensive wartime organization. The great task of putting it on a wartime basis, accumulating the maximum supply of commodities needed for war and adjusting consumption to this, had to be carried out *ab initio*.[2] The government was reluctant to introduce economic regimentation, preferring to work step by step with as much reliance as possible on persuasion and co-operation. Chamberlain's government looked forward to a long defensive war, in contrast to the German policy of a *Blitzkrieg* attack, and relied heavily on the weapon of economic warfare.

The handicap imposed on Great Britain by the completeness of Germany's preparation was balanced to a

[1] New York *Times*, March 20, 1941.
[2] " From a system whose constant aim had been to raise the standard of living it was turned into one whose single purpose was national defence." See W. F. Crick, *An Outline of War-time Financial Control in the United Kingdom* (Macmillan, London, 1941), p. 1.

certain extent by the following facts : Her economy was internally much stronger, because its labour and materials had not already suffered several years of burden imposed by defence economy ; and her higher standard of living constituted a greater reserve for reducing consumption and for increased taxation and saving. Furthermore, conditions were basically more favourable for a considerable increase in production—much labour was unemployed, many plants not fully occupied, and agriculture not developed to its full possibilities.

This situation may explain why the British government thought that the increase of national production and the summoning of the total national effort could be achieved at this stage more effectively through the play of free economic factors than by comprehensive control. British economy was in a position to turn to war purposes the vast reserves of her foreign assets and to enlarge her real war fund by imports—primarily from the Empire. Thus Great Britain could really meet her expenditures in part by a draft on national capital (at home as well as abroad) —a method clearly indicated by use of the term " disinvestment" in the expenditure figures for the first eighteen months of the war. As a financial expedient it is, of course, only temporary ; it conforms to the British conception of the war, which involves the expectation of sufficient time to mobilize democratically the vast resources of the Empire. This conception further assumes unbroken mastery of the seas, since Great Britain, more than any other country, is dependent upon imports of food and raw materials. Both of these assumptions have been seriously challenged.

Britain's economic policy for the war can be divided into three distinct periods : the first up to the invasion of the Low Countries in May 1940, the second lasting approximately throughout the following year and characterized by intensive armament production, and the third beginning with the new budget for 1941-42 and formulated in comprehensive national terms.

The Emergency Powers Act passed on August 24, 1939, authorized the government to take over or control any property or enterprise, but directly forbade industrial conscription. Policy in this first period was determined by the expectation of a long war : democratic forms were to be preserved and the structure of the nation's economic life disturbed as little as possible. Reliance was placed on normal economic mechanisms and the resources of the Empire. Attention was focused primarily on production, but this was organized in an inadequate tempo. National income rose ; consumption was not yet reduced. It does take a certain time to make a democratic people aware of the demands of total war, but it takes time and more time for a dilatory government to develop the attitude and techniques appropriate to the development of a war economy.

Between August 1939 and May 1940 the index of wholesale prices (taking 1930 as 100) rose from 98·1 to 134, or by 36·5 per cent ; the cost of living (July 1914 as 100) rose from 155 to 180, or 16 per cent ; and the index of retail food prices (1914 as 100) rose from 137 to 159, or 15·5 per cent ; average weekly wages rose from 105·75 to 115·75, or 10 per cent. The total number of insured persons unemployed (including those temporarily laid off) was 1,248,000 or 8·7 per cent in August 1939, and went up to 1,766,000 or 10·2 per cent in February 1940 (the best proof that a comprehensive organization of production was lacking) before falling to 890,000 or 6·2 per cent in May 1940.[1]

[1] London and Cambridge Economic Service, *Report on Current Economic Conditions* (February 1941), p. 15.

The rise in prices and in the cost of living (with which wages in important industries are linked) had various causes, chief among them the 14 per cent decline of the pound relative to the dollar. Other factors were the really unusual rise in shipping and insurance rates (railway rates rose following the higher price of coal), the growing war demands, and the rising wage level: none of these was subjected to check. Productive capacities were not yet fully engaged, and the price mechanism was considered an efficient stimulus to production.[1] There was no general control of prices: even the Prices of Goods Act of 1939, effective on January 1, 1940, did not impose real maximum prices. It aimed to stop profiteering and to prevent unreasonable price increases in the goods listed and published by the Board of Trade.[2] Rationing of essential foodstuffs was initiated in January 1940, and applied first to bacon, butter, and sugar, then to meat, tea, and milk. In 1941 rationing was extended to eggs and cheese, jam and marmalade. Various positive measures were of more

[1] It should be noted that the sharpest rise of prices occurred in the first four months of war—September through December 1939: the wholesale price index rose from 98 in August to 122 in December 1939, or 24·4 per cent; the cost of living rose from 155 to 173 or by 11·6 per cent. Afterwards the rising tendency slowed down.

[2] Institute of International Finance, New York, University, *The Danger of Inflation*, p. 114.

The prices of Goods Act prohibits the sale of price-regulated goods at more than the permitted price. The basic price is generally the price charged on August 21, 1939. Increases above the basic price are permitted when they are " reasonably justified in view of changes in the business, since the date as at which the basic price for the goods is to be ascertained ". Under the first order issued by the Board of Trade, prices were fixed for " articles which are widely and necessarily used by large sections of the population ", but this does not include food products (at the outbreak of war increases of prices of the principal foods were prohibited). The whole system is very flexible and it was felt necessary to supplement it in June 1941, by legislation impowering the government to impose maximum prices for various consumer goods.

See Jules Backmann, " War Time Price Control," Contemporary Law Pamphlets, 1940, Series 4, no. 5.

importance. The Ministry of Food became practically the sole importer and buyer of food, handling between £2,000,000,000 and £2,500,000,000 worth of foodstuffs a year.[1] To keep down retail prices of essential foods, a system of subsidies was introduced, rising in amount from £50,000,000 to an estimated £100,000,000 in 1941. To stabilize agricultural prices and at the same time stimulate agricultural production, the government assured the farmer fixed prices on practically all products —grain, sugar, potatoes, milk, livestock. Wages for agricultural workers were raised considerably. The Ministry of Supply became the sole importer and buyer of aluminium, copper, lead, zinc, sulphur, wolfram, pyrites, flax, wool, timber, molasses, and other important materials. Concluding huge contracts (mainly with Empire producers)—some for the duration of the war, some to be renewed annually—it attempted to control and stabilize prices of all raw materials important for war.

The last pre-war budget ended March 31, 1939, closed with the total ordinary revenue of £927,300,000 against expenditures of £940,000,000. In the fiscal year ending March 31, 1940, which included seven months of war, the deficit amounted to £767,000,000. The new greater financial burden was assumed in the budget of April 1940 (the income tax was increased in the first war budget in September 1939 to 7s. 6d. in the pound, and various other taxes also were raised) which nevertheless was from the first regarded as inadequate to its task.

Monetary and credit policy pursued a consistent course. The pound was soon pegged to the dollar on the new parity basis.[2] Foreign exchange was steadily

[1] *War-Time Britain* (British Library of Information, New York), p. 9.

[2] On September 5, 1939, the government carried through a *de facto* stabilization of the sterling. Its value was fixed in relation to gold at 168s. per fine ounce and in relation to the dollar at 4·02-4·06. Paul Einzig, *World Finance*, p. 146.

tightened to utilize all foreign assets for war needs. Foreign exchange and foreign securities, especially American and Canadian, had to be surrendered to a central pool established by the Bank of England and the Treasury. Foreign trade was also controlled. The bank rate was raised on August 24, 1940, to 4 per cent, but was lowered in September to 3 per cent and in October to 2 per cent. A cheap-money policy made it possible for the Treasury to borrow at low rates, and Treasury command of all possible resources supported by co-operation of private banks, was effected by direct and indirect regulation of the flow of capital. The Treasury exercised its supervision over public borrowings to maintain strict control of new issues.

All these measures aimed to reserve the capital market for the state's new borrowing. And according to the *Economist*,[1] of the total of £1,072,200,000 of new issues in 1940, government borrowing represented £1,070,800,000, as against only £1,400,000 of private borrowing. "National Defence Bonds" and "National Saving Certificates" and saving bonds were placed at 3 per cent and National War Bonds at 2·5 per cent; and a new form of cheap short-term borrowing was introduced, i.e. treasury deposits of six months at the rate of $1\frac{1}{8}$ per cent for bank loans. A large-scale campaign also in co-operation with the Post Office Saving Bank for increasing savings especially of small investors was launched very early in order to divert buying power to the state, and as early as February 1940 John Maynard Keynes proposed his plan for compulsory savings in the form of deferred wage and salary payments. This plan was, in modified form, embodied in the budget for 1941-42.[2]

On the whole, we cannot regard this period as already

[1] "Commercial History of 1940," *Economist* (March 15, 1941), pp. 5, 6.
[2] See J. M. Keynes, *How to Pay for the War*, Macmillan, London, 1940.

War Economies 77

a real transition from peace to war economy. Great Britain's wealth in resources has tended to make her underestimate the magnitude of the economic effort involved in total war. National production was unquestionably, but insufficiently, increased. The total increase in national income was less than the increase in state expenditures. National consumption dropped very little.[1] Of course a wealthy economy was in a position to use up a part of its capital in this first period, provided it was doing so with the purpose of achieving greater flexibility and thus greater productivity—in general, a more complete adjustment to war needs.

The invasion of the Low Countries and the defeat of France revolutionized British economic policy. The Bill of May 22, 1940, vested in the government a vast new emergency power, conferring upon it authority to make "provisions requiring persons to place themselves, their services and their property at the disposal of His Majesty as it appears to him to be necessary or expedient". In particular it was intended to empower the government to direct any person to perform any service required,[2] to fix wage rates, hours and conditions of employment, and to inspect premises and employers' records. Munitions production was put directly under government control. Superfluous concerns might be ordered to shut down, subject to reasonable compensation. A special department to stimulate aircraft production was created. The government was thus granted power to institute a

[1] Analysis of expenditures suggests that the nation was at least as well fed in 1940 as in 1938, and that the bulk of the 5 per cent reduction in the standard of living was due mainly to reduced expenditures on clothes and motoring. *Financial News* (April 15, 1941), p. 1.

[2] *War-Time Britain* (British Library of Information, New York, 1940), p. 13. Various important legislative measures are contained in Bulletin No. 116, July 21, 1941, of the Institute of International Finance of New York University in an article: "Some Aspects of British War Economy."

totally administered economy for the duration of the emergency and, especially, also to regulate production, distribution, or consumption of any commodity and to control prices.

But it was still considered preferable to employ all these powers not for regimentation but for strengthening the government's hand in obtaining the necessary voluntary co-operation. The pressure of war made impossible the immediate establishment and development of a comprehensive programme, but war industry had to be mobilized at once, especially in needed armaments like aircraft, tanks, and munitions. Industry was put on a seven-day week, and wherever possible a three-shift day was adopted.

The number of unemployed dropped to 705,000 in December, 1940, and to 581,000 on February 10, 1941; this meant that the proper labour reserve was nearly exhausted. Training of unskilled labour was organized, and in March 1941, all men of 41 and 42 and all women of 20 and 21 were ordered to report for work of national importance. Plans were prepared curtailing in certain industries the right of employers to discharge labour and the right of labourers to change their jobs.[1]

As a whole there was little direct regulation of industry, except for the extension of control over the large number of munitions plants. Supplies of raw material were rationed, production of certain goods (as motor cars) for the home market was prohibited, and sales to retailers in textile and many other goods were limited.

The war effort was accelerated also in the financial field. The expanded budget of July 1940 raised the

---

[1] The Essential Work Order issued in April 1941 has been applied to the merchant marine, to shipbuilding and ship repairing, to coal mining and civil engineering, in order to prevent the exodus of labour from those trades. *Economist* (June 28, 1941), Supplement, p. 5. " British Labour in War-Time," British Library Leaflet, July 30, 1941.

income tax to 8s. 6d. in the pound, or 42·5 per cent, increased taxes on beer, spirits, tobacco and matches, raised postage rates and imposed generally heavier taxation, was the real attempt, though still insufficient, to cope with the situation. In October 1940 a purchase tax of 33⅓ per cent was imposed on wholesale prices of specified luxuries and of 16⅔ per cent on the wholesale price of various personal and household goods. The final deficit for the financial year 1940-41 was £2,475,000,000 against an estimated deficit of £2,100,000,000. (Total ordinary revenue £1,409,000,000 against £3,884,200,000 in total expenditures.)

Prices and wages continued to rise in this period, but more slowly. The index of wholesale prices rose in 1940 from 134 in May to 149 in December, and to 151 in April 1941, or by 12·5 per cent; the cost of living index rose in 1940 from 180 in May, to 195 in December, and to 198 in April 1941, or by 10 per cent; and retail food prices rose from 159 in May to 173 in December, and were 169 in April 1941, or rose by 6·5 per cent. The use of subsidies to keep down prices of basic foods was permanently extended (to bread and flour, home-killed meat and bacon, and milk)—the amount for 1941 being £100,000,000. Price control was also extended and the scheme of maximum prices widened. But the policy still lacked the necessary comprehensiveness.

The upward movement of wages was due in part to their being linked to the index of the cost of living or to the price of some important product. Professor Bowley's index of wages shows an increase from 115¾ in May 1940, to 121¼ in January 1941—5¼ per cent; and total earnings have, of course, risen more.[1]

---

[1] The National wage bill shot up from £1,820,000,000 in 1938 to £2,438,000,000 in 1940—an increase of 36·5 per cent. *Financial News* (April 15, 1941), p. 1. Total earnings have risen nearly 30 per cent (due to overtime pay and increased hours), against the advance of 27 per cent

About two-thirds of total wages are subject to procedures of collective bargaining: both employers' organizations and the trade unions have agreed to bring all disputes before a new National Board whose rulings are binding. The number of working days lost by industrial disputes declined rapidly.

To curtail civilian consumption a system of priorities for raw materials has been adopted; it ranks war industry, production for export, and domestic consumption in that order of preference. Textiles have been directly rationed and the sale of many consumers' goods restricted in various ways. The volume of retail trade for the year ending January 1941 may be inferred from calculations of daily turnover value by the Bank of England: general merchandise was 4·2 per cent higher, food and perishable articles 2·7 per cent, and the general level 3·3 per cent higher.[1] Total stocks on hand were valued at 21 per cent higher than those of a year earlier. These figures, however, must be reduced to take account of the rise in prices, if a real picture of the volume of retail trade is to be obtained.

Total imports in 1940 stood at £1,100,000,000, 24·2 per cent higher than in 1939; total exports were £439,300,000 a drop of 9·5 per cent; and the excess of imports over exports was £660,700,000, a rise of 65·2 per cent. Since May 1940 foreign trade volume has declined in direct ratio to the fall in exports.

In this connection it should be noted that great efforts have been made to increase agricultural production. By the beginning of 1941 more than three and a half million new acres had been put under intensive cultivation, bringing the total to over twelve and a half million acres;

---

in the cost of living index since August 1939 ("British Labour in War-Time").

[1] "Commercial History of 1940," *Economist* (March 15, 1941), p. 29.

and the harvest of 1940 yielded an increase in cereals of one million tons. It is expected that by development of home agriculture, imports of food can be cut from the pre-war 60 per cent to 35 per cent.[1]

In general, the British economy at this time was in full transition from peace to war. Production was increasing, unemployment disappearing, price and wage rises slowing down, consumption being reduced under the impact of extended direct and indirect rationing. The increase in production was not sufficient to meet the increased demand, and a considerable part of war needs were being met out of capital resources abroad and at home. And the opinion still prevailed that the economy was not yet fully mobilized in the fashion required for the waging of total war. I quote from a leading article in the *Economist* to illustrate the difficulties faced by the democratic process in organizing an economy for war. Calling for a vigorous prosecution and co-ordination of war effort, the writer said : " It should no longer be possible for a Chancellor of the Exchequer wilfully to underestimate his task and impose upon the gallant fervour of the voluntary savings movement a labour of Sisyphus. It should no longer be possible for either wages or prices to move in sections out of all relation to the crying needs of the war effort, for extra war earnings to flood depleted markets and for the strategic prices of fuel and transport to rise against every effort to keep the wartime change in values within moderate bounds. It should no longer be possible for men and plants thrown out of work by indispensable war measures to stand idle and useless, while the shadow of a crippling shortage of labour in the war industries not many months from now grows deeper. It should no longer be possible for measures of rationing which are wise as well as expedient

[1] " Bulletins from Britain," *British Library of Information*, May 1941.

to appear too late and reluctantly. It should no longer be possible for antique bogeys—like compulsion, whether of master, man, or saver, all of whom are willing enough if told what to do by the men they have chosen as leaders —to block the path of necessary progress."[1]

The call was generally issued for greater economic effort and for a comprehensive economic war plan.

The demand was answered in the budget for 1941-42, submitted to Parliament in April, and in the war economic programme presented at that time. Simultaneously publication of the whole development of war financing gave entremely valuable information on the structure of the British war economy. I cite below the important figures (see table below).[2]

Total government expenditures in the first war year were covered by revenue, extra-budgetary receipts, and

	Year of September 1939-August 1940	Six months September 1940-February 1941
Total government expenditures in million £	2,597	2,074
Revenues	1,148	837
Draft on external capital[3]	542	479
Draft on domestic capital[4]	60	240
Extra-budgetary receipts	113	90
Increase of tax accruals	140	−20
Savings of local authorities institutions and companies	272	131
Personal savings	320	320
Total income	2,595	2,077

[1] *Economist* (January 11, 1941), p. 32.

[2] See the *Banker* (May 1941), pp. 77-90; *Economist* (April 12, 1941), pp. 475-77; and the White Paper, *An Analysis of the Sources of War Finance and an Estimate of the National Income and Expenditures in 1938 and 1940*, H.M. Stationery Office.

[3] This represents liquidation of foreign assets held by both public funds (mainly by the Exchange Equalization Account) or private owners.

[4] Meaning goods drawn out of stocks and available to the government

increase of tax accruals in the extent of 54 per cent (by revenue alone, of 44·1 per cent), by the draft on capital 23·1 per cent, by personal savings 12·3 per cent, and by other savings 10·4 per cent. In the six months following, revenue, extra-budgetary receipts, and increase of tax accruals covered 43·7 per cent (revenue alone 40·4 per cent), the draft on capital 34·7 per cent, personal savings 15·5 per cent, and other savings 6·4 per cent.

These figures are very significant in their revelation of Britain's economic strength; they go far to dispel the fear of an inflationary "gap", officially defined in economic terms as "the amount of the Government's expenditure against which there is no corresponding release of real resources of man power or materials by some other part of the community". In the first year 77·1 per cent and in the next six months 78·4 per cent of the entire outlay were financed by revenues and the draft on capital, against, respectively, 22·8 per cent and 21·6 per cent by savings.[1] The inflationary "gap" asserted by various analysts was thus limited almost entirely either to that part of savings which can hardly be considered real savings—as they do not result from reduced consumption—or to that part of the draft on capital which was connected with some creation of credit *ad hoc*.

[1] According to a detailed analysis, out of £2,597,000,000 of true government expenditure for the first year of war and of £2,074,000,000 of the first half of the second year, £542,000,000 and £479,000,000 were paid out of overseas sources, so that out of strictly domestic resources were financed £2,055,000,000 and £1,595,000,000. Because of this kind of financing Great Britain obtained goods from abroad without any new domestic purchasing power created in connection with these supplies.

If the goods needed for war are manufactured in the country, government expenditures generate new income, new purchasing power, which has then to be diverted from the market. But if these goods are bought abroad and paid out of existing capital, which must not be converted in consumer incomes, no new purchasing power is created and the whole process has rather anti-inflationary effects, just as for instance the food supplies sent to Great Britain on the Lend-Lease Bill basis.

This use of large capital resources[1] explains the relative lightness of the burden on national income and consumption. The increase of £2,251,000,000 in government expenditure between 1938 and 1940 was attended by a rise of only £1,171,000,000 in net national income; investment of £210,000,000 in 1938 gave way to a net disinvestment of £949,000,000 in 1940—a total difference of £1,159,000,000. This process is well illustrated by the following comparative figures on the various purposes for which the net national income was spent[2]:

	1938	1940 1st quarter	1940 4th quarter
Total net national income	100	100	100
Consumption	77	66	63
Central and local government	19	42	67
Net investment or disinvestment	4	−8	−30
Total consumption in per cent of national income	101	108	130

The net national income for 1940 was estimated at £5,586,000,000, against £4,415,000,000 in 1938. The *Economist* used for this comparison a wider conception of national income—including, besides the net income, total transfer incomes (incomes given without any current returns, interest on national debt, and old age pensions), allowances on depreciation, indirect taxes, and disinvestment of capital (in excess of allowances for depreciation). It thus arrived at a figure—for the total volume of goods and services of all kinds, as well as income and capital available for use—of £7,898,000,000 for 1940, as against £5,948,000,000 for 1938.[3] If this

[1] See Federal Reserve Bulletin (February 1941), pp. 99-101, for an official statement regarding the gold and dollar resources of Great Britain and their use. This put the total amount held on August 31, 1939, at $4,483,000,000, which had because of expenditures of $2,316,000,000 decreased to $2,167,000,000 at the end of December 1940.
[2] *Banker* (May 1941), p. 83.
[3] *Economist* (April 12, 1941), p. 940.

figure is taken as a basis—and it makes possible correlation with the Treasury definition of the inflationary " gap "—the total government expenditure in 1940 was about 42 per cent of available resources (nearly 60 per cent of net income), and only about one-sixth was secured to the government by taxation (about 23 per cent of the net income). Consideration of total available resources makes clearer the psychological pressure, although the real economic burden is more directly indicated by reference to the net national income.

If we analyse the figures regarding the war financing for the period of eighteen months of war from the point of view of deficit and increased state debts, then the government expenditures not covered by budgetary or extra-budgetary receipts represented in the first year of war the amount of £1,336,000,000 and in the period September 1, 1940-February 28, 1941, £1,147,000,000— a total of £2,583,000,000. Proceeds of sale of pre-war resources of the Exchange Equalization Fund brought £388,000,000, and there remained, as the net amount borrowed through sterling loans, £2,095,000,000. An analysis of the forms of sterling public loans was published in the British Government White Paper; a summary of the development is shown in the following table:

	Year Sept. 1, 1939- Aug. 31, 1940	Half Year Sept. 1, 1941- Feb. 28, 1941
	Million Pounds	
Post Office and Trustees Savings banks	82	95
National Saving Certificates	125	83
Defence Bonds	146	84
Other public issues (net)	261	385
Fiduciary issue (increase)	50	—
Treasury bills held at the market (net)	458	−29
Banker's deposit receipts	30	325
	1,152	943
Total		2,095

The nominal value of the total internal national debt on March 31, 1940, was £8,931,000,000 as against £8,027,000,000 a year earlier and against £8,475,000,000 in September 30, 1939. The total debt at March 31, 1941, was £11,400,000,000 or the increase since September 1939 amounted to nearly £3,000,000,000. (Foreign and domestic capital used for the financing of war has been transformed in government bonds.)

The budget for 1941-42 totalled in expenditure £4,207,000,000 (but the estimate was reduced to £3,700,000,000 for total domestic expenditure after the Lend-Lease Bill made unnecessary various payments to the United States). This total is to be made up 44·2 per cent out of ordinary revenues from pre-existing taxation —£1,636,000,000, and 41·1 per cent out of other income such as savings and the draft on capital—£1,522,000,000, with a "gap" of £542,000,000 remaining. This amount, budget experts anticipate, will be covered by new taxation yielding annually £252,000,000 and by further increases of from £200,000,000 to £300,000,000 in personal savings.

Increased tax revenue will come from the income tax, of which the standard rate is raised to 10s. in the pound and on which personal and earned income allowances are reduced, with, moreover, an extension downward to cover two million more taxpayers (increasing the number of taxpayers to twelve million). The direct tax is progressive and goes with the surtax on personal incomes up to a combined maximum of 97·5 per cent. The surtax rate increases to 47·5 per cent on all income over £20,000.[1]

---

[1] The amount of income tax payable reaches the effective rate of 10 per cent on an earned income of £140 for a single person, or £250 for a couple, or £400 for a couple with two children. But a new and very interesting feature of this programme—reminiscent of Keynes's plan of deferred payment, and balancing the reduction in allowances—is the provision for post-war rebates, which the taxpayer will receive after the war in the form of a credit in the Post Office Savings Bank. For instance,

The last budget proposed to estimate expenditures realistically ; and in it no expectation of a large inflationary gap is manifest. The intensity of the war may of course occasion a rise in expenditures, and it may be questioned whether the draft on capital will continue at the same rate or be replaced by foreign credits. In any case, promotion of savings is of increasing importance, both as a source of revenue and as a device for controlling spending and the capital market.

The budget is significant not only from the financial point of view, but also because of its relation to the entire national economic programme. The Treasury was convinced that there will be no inflationary gap, and declared its determination to stabilize, by subsidy where necessary, the prices of all essential goods entering into the cost of living, as well as the cost of essential services such as coal, gas, and electricity. This involves, of course, a national programme for stabilizing wages. The British national policy is now clearly based on the recognition that total war requirements are unlimited,[1] that the total effort must be steadily increased, and that this must in the long run be at the expense of consumption, of the standard of

---

a married couple with two children and an income of £500 pays a tax of £76 and receives a credit of £28. This is a form of compulsory saving which is of considerable political convenience in controlling the spending of the low income group. The total thus saved is estimated at £125,000,000 annually for the duration of the war. This applies obviously to lower incomes, but the scheme of taxation makes it practically impossible for anybody to have more than £3,000 earned income a year.

The Excess Profits Tax of 100 per cent of excess profits provides that one-fifth of all taxes collected shall be returned to the taxpayers at the end of the war on condition of its being used for reconstruction and renovation. This amount is estimated at £35,000,000 a year. The provision aims to stimulate production and to lay a basis for post-war reconstruction, but the company credit when returned will be subject to income tax.

[1] In his speech on July 29, 1941, Prime Minister Churchill said : " We are not a totalitarian state but we are steadily, and I believe as fast as possible, working ourselves into a total war organization," New York *Times*, July 30, 1941, p. 6.

living. The conviction is now apparent that the war economic system must be shifted from a financial basis to one conceived in terms of a real economy of goods and services.

Control of purchasing power aims to divert to the Treasury the maximum of normal market expenditures. This is the purpose of the new income tax; the total of tax revenue may bring in as much as 25 per cent of the national income. Floating of loans—real saving —is again aimed at this goal. The savings campaign had realized by July 1, 1941, a total of subscribed savings certificates, saving bonds and defence bonds of 1,646,617,000, or, for the duration of the campaign, about 15 per cent of the national income. (For the month of May 1941, the total was £197,000,000, for April, £104,100,000, for March, £114,000,000—giving for those three months £425,000,000; this would extend, if continued at the same rate for a year, to about £1,700,000,000 or more than one-fifth of the national income.) Besides that, the 3 per cent war loan brought £302,528,000.

The monthly average of clearing-banks deposits amounted in 1940 to £2,484,000,000, in contrast with an average of £2,248,000,000 in 1939; and the figure for June 1941 reached £2,946,000,000 as against £2,800,000,000 in December 1940.[1] The monthly average of notes in circulation in 1940 was £566,000,000, against £509,900,000 in 1939; at the end of April it reached £621,000,000, and on July 23, 1941, £652,654,817, approaching the present limit of £680,000,000.

---

[1] According to the *Economist* (June 21, 1941), p. 817, the total of bank deposits in the hands of the public has increased by £657,000,000 or 30 per cent over the preceding two years. And in the same two years the increase in the volume of credit placed at the disposal of the Treasury by the clearing bank's holdings of gilt-edged securities, Treasury Bills and Treasury deposit receipts has been about £685,000,000.

The total national debt reached on June 30, 1941, the amount of £12,101,000,000 against £11,394,000,000 on March 31, 1941; that would correspond to a yearly increase of about £3,000,000,000 or much more than was expected. The total increase since September 30, 1939, is about £3,631,000,000. The floating debt as of June 30, 1941, was £3,063,000,000 as compared to £1,167,500,000 at the outbreak of war, and £1,489,000,000 on March 31, 1940. This represented a total increase since the outbreak of war up to June 1941 of £1,895,500,000 against the total increase of state indebtedness of £3,630,000,000, or about 50 per cent.

But the analysis of the expansion of the floating debt since the outbreak of the war shows that a considerable part of this expansion (amounting to £903,220,000) represents the investments of various government funds, especially of the Exchange Equalization Account. Of the remaining £992,250,000, a certain part represents the investment of funds accumulating in London on behalf of Central Banks and issuing authorities in the sterling area. Thus the floating debt in the normal sense really accounts for only a minor part of the total expansion, proving again the non-inflationary policy of the British government and demonstrating clearly the difference in nature and structure of wartime borrowing in Great Britain and Germany up to now.[1]

There is little prospect of a slowing down : government expenditures will continue to grow, are currently running at £12,000,000 a day, and the savings at the rate of £5,500,000 a day are not enough to bridge the " true inflationary gap ".[2] The Exchequer returns for the first

---

[1] *Economist* (July 5, 1941), p. 16.

[2] The Chancellor of the Exchequer in the Commons on June 24, 1941. *Economist* (June 28, 1941), p. 848.
Ordinary expenditure for the week ended June 14, 1941, reached

quarter of the financial year 1941-42 (April 1-June 30) show the total ordinary revenue as £319,158,000 and total ordinary expenditure as £1,074,281,000, or a deficit of £755,123,000, which has to be covered by borrowing.

The necessity of more savings is apparent, but the rise in money incomes caused by increased production will not suffice to make easier a great increase in voluntary savings. The problem of thoroughgoing price control at all key points like basic foods, rent, fundamental clothing, coal, transport, steel, gas and electricity, and of wage control accompanied by some form of statutory limitation on consumption will necessarily recur. The index of wholesale commodity prices advanced from 151·3 in May, 1941 to 152·4 in June, the largest increase since December 1940, making the aggregate increase since the war began 55 per cent, the rise in food prices being 60 per cent and in industrial material 53 per cent. The average rise in the level of weekly full time rates of wages between September 1, 1939, and June 1, 1941, was about 20 per cent.[1] The official cost of living index rose in the same time by 29 per cent.

We may therefore expect a further step towards more comprehensive control of prices, wages, and consumption, combined with intensified savings campaigns in order to limit the danger of inflation.

But there is no movement in the Stock Exchange similar to that in Germany. The index of common

---

a total of £83,946,000 and for the week ended June 21, £87,749,000, against ordinary revenues of £19,345,000 and £25,902,000 respectively.

The expenditures reached £12,000,000 daily, against £6,000,000 estimated at the beginning of the war; the value of Lend-Lease deliveries is, of course, not included.

[1] Quoting Mr Bevin, Minister of Labour, in the House of Commons on June 26, *Financial News* (London, June 27, 1941), pp. 1, 2. But see also footnote 1, page 79, on the increase of total earnings.

stocks shows a considerable stability, the level being still below the pre-war prices. The index was in August 1939, 75·3 ; in January 1940, 75·7 ; in June 1940 (defeat of France), 64·9 ; in December 1940, 70·2 ; July 1941, 75·4. On the other hand the index of bonds reached 121·7 in April 1941, against 110·9 in August 1939 ; 117·6 in January 1940 ; 113·4 in June 1940, and 121 in December 1940.

Insistent demands are heard for the pooling of technical and financial resources in industry, mining, and agriculture, under direct state control.[1]

Mobilization of industrial production is proceeding more rapidly. Labour reserves have been practically exhausted (the number of unemployed in April 1941 was 411,000, and on May 12, 368,988 and 278,280 in July. The government has initiated a two-year conscription of male and female labour which must clearly be incorporated into a large-scale demobilization of labour in non-essential industries if production is to be further increased and civilian production and consumption reduced. At the end of July 1941 it was announced that three million men and women will be required to register for essential war work between August 2 and December 6. (The women born between the years 1910 and 1916 and the men born in 1895, 1896, 1897, have to register now.)

In order to economize on labour it will be necessary to concentrate the production of civilian goods in a limited number of nucleus plants. In March 1941 the Board of Trade developed schemes to induce private firms to co-operate on a basis at once appropriate to war needs and to a fair adjustment of their position after the war.[2]

---

[1] *New Statesman and Nation* (London, April 12, 1941), p. 379 ; and *Economist* (May 31, 1941), p. 729.

[2] Thomas P. Wilson, " British Concentration of Production," *Foreign Commerce Weekly* (June 14, 1941), p. 447.

The concentration of the consumption goods industries was expected to release 500,000 to 700,000 men and women for war work.[1] These plans are further supported by increasing rigidity in the allocation of raw material supplies and rationing of consumption (as in clothes). The economy in the second half of the second year of war has been brought to full mobilization of production in conformity with the demands of war. To satisfy these demands a decline in civilian consumption—in the standard of living—is inevitable. But to avoid and limit inflation Britain must institute a comprehensive financial policy embracing definite supervision of prices and wages. It is a matter of political import to determine whether co-operation or compulsion is more suitable to carry this out.

The great resources of Great Britain and the Empire make possible a further draft on national capital. Real income from foreign sources, i.e. the Lend-Lease Bill and contributions from the Commonwealths, enlarges the real war fund of Great Britain and shifts the war burden from country to country and perhaps from generation to generation.

The impact of total war on developed national economies is so severe and intense that it is generally under-estimated until after the time for meeting it effectively. Total warfare imposes demands that are practically limitless and lead to the exhaustion of all economic resources. A definite pattern of effects, fundamental in character, is discernible in the national economy, whether it be totalitarian or democratic. For

---

[1] This process of concentration has made the greatest advance in the textile industry. About 180 spinning mills have been closed out of 415 in the trade, and some 150 weaving firms out of about 1,000 sheds will cease production the next time. *Economist* (June 18, 1941), Trade Supplement, p. 5.

economic strategy is one of the most important implements of modern war, and democracies find that they must not only match the military weapons of totalitarian aggressors but also organize effectively to develop the economic necessities for war. Transformation from peace to an adequate war economy can be accomplished only through a comprehensive national plan.

The primary necessity is satisfaction of the war demands, which are of such volume as to require, in addition to an increase in national production, a drastic cut in civilian consumption, and a fall in the standard of living below what has been anticipated. The importance of the real problem of mobilizing national labour, resources, and production has tended to eliminate purely monetary considerations and to promote thinking and planning in terms of the real economy. Money has become merely auxiliary to the organization of the war economy—an aid in distributing its sacrifices and effects, but not in itself a motive for economic activities. On the other hand, this war, unlike other great wars, has been financed up to now on both sides with the definite intention of preventing further inflation. As Keynes put it, " Germany has stopped it dead, and we have stopped it largely. It [preventing inflation] is a thing you must do. It is perfectly possible. There is no reason in the world why not. It's just a muddle and there is no need to have a muddle."[1]

It is a question of organization, which becomes more and more difficult as government expenditures come to absorb 50-60 per cent of the net national income (which is, of course, not identical with all available resources).[2]

[1] New York *Times* (May 9, 1941), p. 1.

[2] It must be recalled in this connection that the German government borrows more heavily from savings deposits in banks than does the British ; in Great Britain, a much larger part of new state loans is absorbed by the owners of savings. Purchasing power in Great Britain is transferred

The government must steadily divert to the Treasury the excess purchasing power of all incomes, and especially that of the smaller incomes which have been swelled by war expenditures. Here, clearly, is a levelling tendency. The public will demand equality of sacrifices; war must not be good business for anybody. At the same time, the public will experience a steady expansion of state control in all fields of economic activity. And it is a question whether it will be possible in a long war absorbing such a large proportion of national income to organize permanently national economy in such a way as to avoid inflationary effects unless an organization similar to a natural economy is established.[1]

Germany entered the war with a fully organized and mobilized war economy, whereas it took Great Britain twenty months from the war's beginning to approximate the same status. The British, however, started with greater resources and financial reserves; they could meet war expenses partly through drafts on capital, and thus lessen the strain on national income. The British economy has been and remains more flexible, more internally dynamic, and more securely founded on public co-operation.

But the economic impact of total war involves some demands which all governments must meet. Even free welfare economies must adopt some measure of central organization. The extent to which the state can defer

---

more directly from the consuming public to the government, whereas in Germany it is deposited first in banks. Therefore the Germans face a much greater danger that hidden inflation may suddenly become open inflation. They can prevent it only through post-war control of consumption, which would be very difficult politically and psychologically.

[1] The *Economist* (May 3, 1941, p. 580) asks for still greater efforts and a more effective economic organization: "The ideal financial policy for totalitarian war would therefore be to guarantee an income to every citizen, unconnected with the work he does; to call on him to do any work that is required; and completely to control what he could consume."

compulsion in favour of persuasion and voluntary co-operation is a matter of psychology and relative efficiency. The earlier the economy is adjusted to full wartime efficiency the smaller will be the ultimate loss. If we compare the German and the British war economy, we find indeed a great similarity, despite a different degree of regimentation and commandeering : in both countries there is the policy of financing the war without inflationary effects, with taxation absorbing a great portion of national income ; in Germany a general freezing of prices and wages, in Great Britain a steadily expanding control of prices supported by various indirect devices. In both countries we see reduction of non-defence production in order to release labour for war production, lack of skilled labour and also the conscription-registration of workers (which, of course, was initiated in Germany long ago). Further, there is rationing of consumption in both countries ; in Germany this is comprehensive, in Great Britain more elastic and also working by indirect controls ; in both there is great liquidity on the money and capital markets, but whereas the index of common stocks in Great Britain is below the pre-war level, the increase of common stock prices in Germany reflects clearly an inflationary nervousness.

Germany, although better prepared and organized at the beginning, was forced to rely relatively soon on strengthening and completing her resources by means of conquest and the economic exploitation of conquered territories. Economic necessities doubtless influenced her military programme. Great Britain also must count on support and deliveries from abroad, and is fortunate in being able to call upon the British Commonwealth and the Lend-Lease aid of the United States. Of course, the time factor and transportation problems must not be neglected.

A totalitarian war economy, thoroughly organized, cannot win the war if it is not backed by real economic strength ; on the other hand it is equally true that a democratic economy, even with the mightiest resources, cannot prevent losing the war if it remains on the welfare economy basis and is not organized quickly and efficiently.

DEFENCE PROGRAMME IN THE UNITED STATES

A detailed examination of the defence economy of the United States is impossible here ; we shall limit discussion to some of the more important problems. The extraordinarily strong economic position of this country, the size of its war potential, the high degree of self-sufficiency possible and the relatively insubstantial dependence on importation of strategic materials, the equipment and capacity of industry, the reserves of national income and the relatively light fiscal burden (as compared with European countries)—these factors could easily produce over confidence in regard to the organization of economy to satisfy defence needs.

In the first year of the war American defence industry began to produce, in the main, goods for delivery to France and England. The effect of these exports on American economy was similar to the usual multiplier-effect of increased production, although it was distributed among a limited number of industries and although it caused some dislocation by changing the composition of total export. However, since it was only a very small fraction of the total volume of production, this disturbance presented no serious problem.

When the real defence programme began (contract awards in the three months June-August 1940, aggregated $2,000,000,000) many plants were still only partially occupied, large amounts of funds idle, and much labour unemployed. Thus the defence programme was often discussed from the point of view of extending production and employment and increasing the national income. How could the multiplier possibilities in defence production best be used to stimulate the country's economic activity as a whole?[1]

It was believed that the American economy could meet defence requirements without having to reduce normal production—that guns and butter could be had at the same time. (Some, theorizing from a general multiplier-effect, expected guns and *more* butter.) It was pointed out that Nazi Germany had been able to manufacture tremendous quantities of armaments and at the same time to raise national consumption above the low level of 1932.[2] But the timing and the size of the programme are important. Germany, preparing aggression and not faced by the necessity of immediate defence, could inaugurate and carry forward the military measures at such time and rate as she considered wise. She was able systematically to adjust all the details of national production to one goal.

At the beginning of the first year of the war, defence appropriations in the United States were brought into a mechanical relationship with the total national income and volume of national production; and it seemed obvious that such a small fraction of the total could easily

---

[1] See, for instance, Robert V. Rosa, "A Multiplier Analysis of Armament Expenditure," *American Economic Review* (June 1941), pp. 219-65.

[2] According to Staudinger and Lehmann (Conference Board Economic Record, 1940, p. 308), the increase in German national income in the six and a half years between Hitler's rise to power and the beginning of the war is estimated at 133,000,000,000 reichsmarks. Two-thirds of this increase—or 90,000,000,000 reichsmarks—was spent on armament; the remaining 43,000,000,000 reichsmarks is the increase in income available for consumption. But because many items actually produced for military purposes are not included in this 90,000,000,000, I regard the figure of 43,000,000,000 remaining as too high. The real increase was much lower, although it still provided a slight margin over the extremely low income of 1932.

be manufactured over and above existing production and that no widespread adjustments or limitations would be necessary. (National income in 1940 was $74-75,000,000,000; defence expenditures for the fiscal year ending June 1941 amounted to $6,050,000,000.) No measures were contemplated that might brake expanding production or rising consumption.

We have already discussed the structure of armament demand and the related civilian demand, and we have mentioned the problem of the technical and labour bottlenecks operating to limit increasing production.[1] To overcome these difficulties, labour is to be trained, new plants built, existing plants extended, etc. The task can easily be completed within the resources of this country's economy if there is time enough for it and if the new demand preserves a reasonable ratio to total demand. But there is the further question of how much expansion is necessary and desirable and of how fully total capacity should be employed in the light of probable post-war difficulties. (Of course, the whole problem changes with time pressure and increasing production for defence.)

By July 1941 total appropriations and contract authorizations under the defence programme amounted to about $47,000,000,000 (including British government orders the aggregate exceeded $50,000,000,000). Cash expenditures under this broad programme, including British government orders, have been running in July at the rate of $1,100,000,000 a month[2] and at an annual rate of about $13,000,000,000. This is 15·29 per cent of an estimated national income of $85,000,000,000[3] or

[1] Some very interesting details in connection with American war economy can be found in J. Philipp Wernette's article " Guns and Butter " in the *Harvard Business Review* (Spring 1941), pp. 286-97.
[2] Federal Reserve Bulletin (August 1941), p. 724.
[3] Alvin H. Hansen, *Fiscal Policy and the Business Cycle* (W. W. Norton, New York, 1941), p. 429; and Federal Reserve Bulletin (August 1941), p. 724.

14·88 per cent of an income of $88,000,000,000 (according to the national income payments by June 1941). Present plans call for an expenditure of $11,000,000,000 in the second half of 1941 and of $22,000,000,000 in 1942, but even this figure may be increased.[1] An armament expenditure of $22,000,000,000 would amount to 25 per cent of the national income, which is estimated at $85-90,000,000,000 for 1942. The percentage may be higher as a result of price developments and intensified defence production. At any rate, it is clearly illustrated that defence spending increases faster than the total national production and income; the United States has experienced less disproportion than did European countries in the first years of their military preparations. "The attempt to superimpose defence efforts on peacetime production" cannot be carried out successfully. Production could not be extended rapidly enough or in sufficient volume to satisfy armament requirements in this way; in this country, as in the others, it will be found possible to prepare adequate defence only by reducing production and consumption of civilian goods. Such reduction can be more easily carried out in an economy like that of the United States, which can continue to supply the more important daily commodities. But some sacrifices in consumption will be necessary; their extent and structure will largely depend on the volume and the urgency of the defence requirements.

As it was once advisable to refrain from restrictive and controlling measures in order to permit development of the national economy to an equilibrium and an optimum output, so it is now desirable that the defence programme establish a national economic policy in order

[1] Stacy May, Chief of the Bureau of Research and Statistics of the Office of Production Management, in the New York *Herald-Tribune* (June 2, 1941), p. 1.

to prevent a general inflationary rise in prices. Such policy requires *a co-ordinated financial and price-and-wage programme combined with a comprehensive priority system.* The strength of the American economic position makes less difficult the necessary adjustment of production and consumption ; and the methods of persuasion and public co-operation, if the people are united in their support of government policy, can be used to a large extent. But it must be recognized—in contradiction to the opinion prevailing a year ago—that the success of the defence programme, the volume of which may suddenly increase even further, involves such an adjustment. Despite full employment and largely increased total national production and monetary income and also the fact that the nation is not engaged actively in war, the standard of living cannot rise and consumption has to be adjusted to the general situation. Total war means great sacrifices, and if a state of emergency exists so that its demands cannot be satisfied according to a definite long-period plan, civilian consumption and even real national income must suffer. For it is contrary to the nature of total war that a nation, either in preparing for it or waging it, should feel no pressure on the standard of living. A state which is forced to adopt destructive measures in order to preserve its freedom must be prompt to toil and sacrifice.

CHAPTER IV

ECONOMIC WARFARE

PERIOD UP TO THE DEFEAT OF FRANCE

THE British and French conception of the war found clear expression in their economic strategy. They planned for a long war rather than the *Blitzkrieg* which German theorists had worked out and explained many times over. The Allies were convinced that the German economy could not support a long war; they attached supreme importance to economic warfare—to a static as against a dynamic conception of the war. In this they relied upon various official and many more unofficial analyses of Germany's economic resources and upon the expectation that Germany could not—despite her pre-war policy of autarchy—reach an adequate degree of self-sufficiency. The weaknesses in the German system would develop, it was thought, if the supply of foodstuffs and raw materials could be cut off—though in this the Allies showed themselves imperfectly informed on Germany's preparations to meet the impact of the blockade.

An official British publication in the first months of the war asserted: "However large a nation's armies and navies may be, it cannot carry on the fight without certain key resources—food for the people and raw materials for its factories. Because of our command of the seas, we can continue to draw vital materials from every part of the world. The Nazis, on the other hand, must sooner or later find themselves in great difficulties."[1] And the same source pointed out in enumerating Germany's deficiencies that she depends upon imports

[1] *Assurance of Victory* (Ministry of Information, H.M. Stationery Office, London, 1939), p. 19.

for two-thirds of her peacetime oil consumption (totalling about 7,000,000 tons), for two-thirds of the necessary iron ore (about 18-20,000,000 tons), and for nearly half of the required fats.

Many detailed analyses were offered to show Germany's economic weakness. It was stated, and correctly, that, of the thirty-four raw materials absolutely indispensable for war, Germany possessed adequate stocks of only four; of the remaining thirty, she depended on imports in part for seven and entirely for twenty-three.[1] The main deficiencies were calculated on the basis of accepted figures for production, consumption, and foreign trade, as well as on estimated consumption during the war. The more important of these follow.[2]

Iron ore imports in 1938 amounted to 21,900,000 tons, of which Sweden provided 41 per cent, France 23 per cent, Luxembourg 8 per cent, Newfoundland, Norway and Spain together 5 per cent and Greece, Rumania and Africa the rest. About 900,000 tons of fats or 45 per cent of total consumption were imported, in both animal and vegetable form. Home production of copper met only 8 per cent of requirements, which were already on a wartime basis, and of lead only 40 per cent of the very pressing demand. The German position in zinc was more favourable, with 70 per cent of the needs supplied from domestic mines. But Germany depended entirely on imports for tin, chromium, tungsten, nickel, molybdenum, and other metals; requirements for phosphates for fertilizers could be satisfied from domestic production only to 40 per cent or 45 per cent. For rubber Germany had to rely mostly upon synthetic production, and a

[1] Ivan Lajos, *Germany's War Chances* (Victor Gollancz, London, 1939), p. 106.
[2] See also Hellmut von Rauschenplat and Hilda Monte, *How to Conquer Hitler* (Jarrolds, London, 1940), pp. 68-138; and D. T. Jack, *Studies in Economic Warfare* (P. S. King & Son, London, 1940), pp. 146-68.

similar situation obtained for wool, cotton, other textile materials, and for all colonial products, including coffee, tea, and most of her tobacco.[1] The general problem presented by oil has been mentioned: it should be added that heavy lubricating oils constituted an especially difficult problem. Consumption of lubricating oils for Germany, Austria, and Czechoslovakia was estimated at 700,000 tons annually; domestic production, only a little supplemented from Rumania, did not exceed 400,000 tons and was seriously lacking in heavy oils.

I shall not go on to enumerate all the products in respect of which Germany depended on imports. Enough has been said to support the general belief that Germany was not prepared in economic terms for a long war, and that the Allies had reason to count heavily upon their economic supremacy. But the analysis is incomplete without some additional explanations and qualifications. As I have stated above, the volume of arms and equipment accumulated in the German effort of preparation for war was generally underestimated. So were her stocks of important raw materials of all kinds, especially of oils and metals, despite the general knowledge that she had purchased these in huge amounts even in the months preceding the war. Again, consumption of such materials was very often calculated on the basis of the first World War experience, which was marked by all-out war of tremendous proportions on long-standing fronts. On this basis estimates of oil consumption ran from twelve to thirty million tons a year.[2] Too little consideration was given to the flexibility of consumption in a controlled

[1] Cleona Lewis, *Nazi Europe and World Trade*, Brookings Institution, Washington, 1941.

[2] Louis E. Frechtling, in "Oil and the War," *Foreign Policy Reports* (June 1, 1941), p. 77, estimates consumption of oil in the Polish campaign at probably two or three million barrels and in the Battle of France only at ten million barrels.

war economy, where a maximum pressure can be applied to effect a reduction, and to the squeezing of other states for the necessary supplies. Nor was the extent of Germany's use of substitutes fully understood. Finally, the blockade proved less effective than that of the first World War: fewer states were engaged in war; the German frontier remained open to the east and south; and Germany did not passively accept the encirclement of her boundaries.

The conquest of Poland made Germany self-sufficient in zinc and supplemented her resources of fats and potatoes. It further provided her with ample supplies of coal to use as a barter medium for trade in other necessary commodities, over and above large accessions in armaments and other stocks.[1] Germany could further improve her position by calling upon the neutral European countries. Export surplus of cereals in Hungary, Yugoslavia, and Rumania exceeded German imports of these materials. Imports from the neutral countries represented 81 per cent of German imports of cattle, 100 per cent of hogs, 94 per cent of butter, 81 per cent of eggs, 84 per cent of cheese, 87 per cent of vegetables; all these could be increased if necessary. (The chief European exporters to Germany of dairy products and vegetables were Denmark and Holland; of iron ore and wood pulp, Sweden; of oil, Rumania and Russia; of manganese ore, Russia; of zinc, copper, lead, chromium, antimony pyrites, and bauxite, Yugoslavia; of bauxite, Hungary; of chromium, Turkey; of pyrites, Greece; of various minerals, Norway.)[2] Since the beginning of her preparation for war, German effort had been concentrated on

[1] Poland in recent years exported annually 500,000 tons of grain, 60,000 tons of meat, 11,000 tons of butter, and 26,000 tons of eggs. Rauschenplat and Monte, *How to Conquer Hitler*, p. 39.

[2] "Germany's Bid for Self-Sufficiency," *Financial News* (May, 1939), London.

the all-important basic supplies of iron ores, fats, and oils. Her economic position as a whole, even for a long war, was thus stronger than in 1914.

Against Germany the Allies waged an economic war that was better prepared than were some other elements in their economic strategy. Following the experience of the last war, they employed principally the weapons of blockade, boycott, and concentrated pre-emptive purchases.[1] Great Britain immediately established a special ministry of economic warfare, and a similar organization was set up in France. On September 4, 1939, a list of absolute and conditional contraband was proclaimed in Great Britain, and on November 27, 1939, an Order in Council authorized the seizure of German exports on the high seas. Full naval blockade was thus instituted, aiming to prevent importation of all goods to Germany—whether direct or indirect—and to cripple Germany's effort to maintain her foreign buying power by overseas exports. The naval blockade on the flow of war supplies into Germany soon became effective; and thereby imposed an early pressure on her resources. A system of compulsory "navicerts" was, after some months, imposed on all ships entering European and North African harbours, replacing the requirement that all such shipping put in at contraband control ports for inspection and confiscation of contraband goods.

The Allies' complete sea control enabled them to make the direct blockade really effective. There remained, of course, the problem of the trade of neutral countries. In the last war a great intermediary trade, carefully camouflaged, had passed through these states, evading the blockade and bringing Germany supplies. As this device was again employed, the Allies faced the difficult

[1] For various legal aspects of the blockade, see D. T. Jack, *Studies in Economic Warfare*.

task of controlling the imports of neutrals, who thus came under pressure from both sides. The Allies' effort to curtail their imports was set against Germany's demand for the greatest possible supply of goods. Britain declared on September 14, 1939, that " It is the object of the British contraband control to prevent cargoes of contraband from being imported into Germany, whether directly or through neutral countries ". This was clearly a retort to the statement by an official German source the previous day that the " German government makes it clear that it would consider it an unneutral attitude if the neutral states allowed others to subject them to actual restrictions or formal control aimed against the normal exchange and transit of goods between neutral countries and Germany ".

But the task of the blockade was not only to prevent actual German importation, direct and indirect. It was further to keep the neutral countries from increasing production of important raw materials for export to Germany. So, for example, Denmark and the Netherlands had to import large quantities of fodder in order to maintain an export of dairy products to the Reich; Belgium and Switzerland imported various metals for re-export in some modified form to Germany. It was therefore necessary to work out with the neutral countries some scheme for supplying their requirements. This was generally based upon their consumption for the last years preceding the war, but the Allies made liberal allowances for the importation of stocks for reserve, subject to a guarantee that these would not be re-exported.[1]

The blockade technique improved steadily, but large loopholes persisted. One was the traffic from the Far East via the trans-Siberian railway; another and more

[1] R. W. B. Clarke, *Britain's Blockade*, Oxford Pamphlets on World Affairs, 1941, p. 9.

important one was Italy. In the latter case the Allies continued to try by appeasement to forestall Italian entry into the war. Failing any serious attempt at blockade, a steady supply of various goods went to Germany through Italy, and in the contrary direction Italy was used by Germany to camouflage the export of many German goods.

Britain was able, indeed, to rely upon a world-wide organization of trade and finance. Following the Trading with the Enemy Act she issued a black list of firms operating in German spheres of influence or under German control : all business with them was prohibited, regardless of their nationality. The list includes more than three thousand firms in all parts of the world—a great many in South America. Furthermore, British participation in a number of important companies supplying the world's markets in raw materials enabled her to exercise efficient control of these materials at their source.

It was far more difficult to interfere with German imports from continental Europe. Germany was able to profit by the economic domination which she had developed in south-eastern Europe before the war and to extend that even further. She possessed a better commercial organization, she bought up all available quantities of goods, regardless of price or quality, and, surprisingly, showed herself better able to deliver goods rapidly and in great quantities than were the Allies. She was even able to supply other countries with the armament which was urgently demanded, though in part this turned out to be captured Polish or Czechoslovak material. In compensation for the reduction in overseas trade, she concentrated all her attention on the Continent and substantially extended the volume of trade there. She was also able to reduce her debit balances on many clearing accounts. Economic factors and military pressure thus combined to produce for Germany a very favourable bargaining relation with Continental Europe. Only in the Low Countries and Scandinavia, which depended directly on overseas imports, could the Allies offer serious competition. Even there the menace of complete German domination did not stir the small neutral countries to ally themselves with Great Britain and France and to support their economic policy. The issue of appeasement and of years of disunity was apparent in the declining prestige of the Western Democracies.

To implement her struggle for important commodities in south-eastern Europe, Great Britain established at the beginning of 1940 a special official company, the United Kingdom Commercial Corporation. Its task was to intensify British trade with the Balkan countries by means of pre-emptive purchases, and thereby to curtail the flow of many commodities to Germany. The German policy of paying prices above those in the world market was imitated. Though rather slow to initiate this type of economic offensive, Great Britain enjoyed the advantage of holding important raw materials like rubber, jute, tin, cotton, and all colonial products; these she was able to offer in exchange for goods that it was important to divert from Germany. By raising the prices of these raw materials she could facilitate payment of higher prices for Balkan commodities. She also attempted to answer the demand of these countries for armament and for financial assistance: a special loan was made to Turkey in January 1940 to the amount of £40,000,000, of which £25,000,000 was to go into armament.[1]

The economic offensive was developed on a broad scale and in direct conflict with German policy. Diversion from

[1] Paul Einzig, *World Finance, 1939-1940* (Kegan Paul, London, 1940), p. 229.

Germany of Rumanian oil was attempted in the face of the Rumanian Government's guarantee to Germany of an annual delivery of 1,400,000 tons. Offers of special import favours were explicitly conditioned by restrictions on specified exports to Germany from the countries affected; the Balkan countries responded reluctantly as far as they dared. The conflict was sharpest in oil, iron ores, and fats. And it was certainly in large part the menace of the blockade to the supply of the vital high-grade Swedish ores (two-thirds of which were shipped via Narvik) that speeded up Germany's resort to military operations. At the moment when the economic warfare began to work in full strength Germany answered by military action. And thus it can be said that the economic warfare began to be really effective and compelled Germany to take military action and risk which she otherwise would have preferred to avoid.

The German military successes did much to complicate Great Britain's economic war problems. Denmark, Norway, the Low Countries, and France were conquered and occupied, and Germany became economic master of continental Europe. The Balkans, with the possible exception of Turkey, became practically closed to British influence: even before the military occupation they had been forced to accommodate their economies to German demands. Countries with agricultural surpluses like Hungary, Rumania, and Yugoslavia were compelled to ration domestic food consumption in order to increase deliveries to Germany. Dutch and British oil companies in Rumania and British mining companies in Yugoslavia were forced to supply Germany with oil, zinc, lead, and pyrites. The British tactic of economic war was thus profoundly handicapped by German domination of the Continent, and by the German counter blockade of the British Isles by submarines and aircraft.

AFTER THE FRENCH ARMISTICE

Great Britain's dependence on overseas imports was very seriously increased by the German victories. About 30 per cent of British imports had come from the Continent; the following table shows specifically how the importation of various goods was affected[1]:

GREAT BRITAIN'S IMPORTS OF CERTAIN PRODUCTS IN 1938

Product	Total imports (in 1,000 metric tons)	From Europe (except U.S.S.R.)
Pork	450·2	311·5
Butter	488·1	206·9
Cheese	137·9	16·3
Eggs	148·2	117·9
Wheat	5,142	763
Refined sugar	52·4	37·1
Flax	57·1	33·1
Bauxite	197·6	190·8
Iron ore	4,621	2,519
Iron and steel	271·9	230·7
Scrap	444·7	203·4
Sulphur	87·3	32·8
Wood (conifers) in 1,000 m.³	13,517	8,305
(others) ,, ,,	1,682	509
Wood pulp (mechanical)	618·2	598·2
(chemical)	844	833

Great Britain was forced to replace her imports from Europe by goods from remote countries overseas and to impose a tremendously increased burden upon her merchant marine and navy. The effort of the blockade was thus doubled by the task of assuring Britain's supplies —to say nothing of the loss of the French fleet, a loss only partially offset by the addition of Norwegian, Belgian, and Dutch shipping. The problem of blockading Germany has, of course, been in a manner simplified: the blockade is now extended to practically the entire Continent. Domination of the seas has become increasingly important.

[1] *Europe's Trade* (League of Nations, Geneva, 1941), pp. 108, 109.

In examining the economics of the German and Italian situation after the French armistice, we must distinguish between the immediate conditions of the war and a long view. It is obvious that the structure of Europe's economy, and especially that of western Europe, has not changed: the whole area remains committed to an exchange of its industrial goods for raw materials and foods from overseas. German deficiencies in these respects have increased—particularly in oil, rubber, textile raw materials, colonial products, copper, tin, lead, and other minerals. The recent publication by Cleona Lewis[2] gives the following figures: net imports of foods to Nazi Europe in 1937 were valued at $648,200,000, and of raw materials at $2,594,700,000, amounting together to $3,242,900,000. Specifically, Nazi Europe's deficiency in copper was between 67 per cent and 75 per cent, in lead about 50 per cent, in tin about 90 per cent, in rubber 100 per cent, in oil more than 67 per cent, in fats almost 40 per cent, and in cereals about 10 per cent. The implication is clear of the dependence of any internationally co-operative European economy on world trade; of this any plan for future European organization must take cognizance. Immediately, the question is how far the conquest and domination of Europe can support the German conduct of the war.

Germany has prepared a blueprint of the procedure for organizing a conquered territory so as to exploit to the full its resources for carrying on the war. A special department of the War Economy and Armament Board of the High Command has specified these provisions in the necessary detail. The plan includes requisitioning of

[2] *Nazi Europe and World Trade*, p. 78. The countries included here in a Nazi Europe are: Albania, Austria, Belgium-Luxemburg, Bulgaria, Czechoslovakia, Denmark, France, Germany, Greece, Hungary, Italy, The Netherlands, Norway, Poland, Portugal, Rumania, Spain, Sweden, Switzerland and Yugoslavia.

finished products as well as of raw materials, the gearing of industries into the German war industry programme, and where desirable the transfer of machines to Germany. "Wherever stocks of materials or finished goods could be traced down, the sign 'Confiscated by the Army High Command' had to be at once put up; and not a single piece was lost thereafter."[1] The conquest of all these countries, recently supplemented by Yugoslavia and Greece, has brought an enormous booty.[2] The German war chest has been thus replenished by great supplies of oil, rubber, metals, textile raw materials, food, and the armament supplies of nearly the entire Continent. There were correlative difficulties, such as the decline of stocks of cattle, hogs, and poultry consequent on fodder deficiencies in Holland and Denmark : while supplies of food and fats rose for the immediate present, the sources of future supplies were reduced. The fact that this constituted a draft on substance did not change the immediate situation—as it was if Germany had increased her present supply of metals by dismantling factories in occupied countries.

In addition to immediate gains of such economic booty, the German economy has acquired support in the wholesale organization of the economies of the conquered states to accord with the war effort. The whole Continent has been in effect organized on the basis of a regimented war economy. Production and consumption have to be adjusted and limited as it best suited the German war needs. Berlin has become owner or acquired control of all important industrial enterprises and banks and has reorganized monetary systems in such a way as to permit

[1] Hans Baumgarten in *Der Deutsche Volkswirt* (October 18, 1940), pp. 94, 96, in the article "The New Weapon".

[2] See, for instance, Antonín Basch, *Germany's Economic Conquest of Czechoslovakia* (Czechoslovak National Council of America), Chicago, 1941.

the German Government to trade entirely in terms of marks. The relation between the mark and other national currencies has been fixed on the basis of a fictitious gold parity (in November 1940 the mark was again proclaimed equal to the gold mark), giving Berlin the opportunity to buy very cheaply with over-valued marks and to inflate the monetary systems of the occupied countries.

A multilateral clearing system for intra-European trade has been organized, with its centre in Berlin. Difficulties of payment in such trade have thus been " eliminated ", as Berlin decides what payments may and may not be cleared, and accordingly manipulates the balance for her own best advantage. She has, in a word, mobilized for her war needs all the resources of continental Europe.

The industrial potential at Germany's command has increased substantially. To the German and Czech armament works have been added the French, Belgian, and Dutch. Iron and steel capacity is now estimated at from 35,000,000 to 42,000,000 tons annually, compared with the 17,000,000 tons of the British Empire and the 90,000,000 tons of the United States.[1] Production of aluminium, of which Germany alone can produce 180,000 to 200,000 tons annually, may reach 300,000 tons when the production of French, Italian, Norwegian, and Swiss works is included ; and the supply of bauxite is ample. There are surpluses in magnesium, wood pulp, paper production, and mercury. The chemicals industry, already highly developed, has been enlarged. Germany has without doubt continued to build up armament. The pre-war effort to strengthen her economic basis by extension of the substitutes industry has certainly gone

[1] See Louis Domeratzky, " The Industrial Power of the Nazis," Vol. 19, No. 2. *Foreign Affairs* (April 1941), pp. 641-54.

forward. Synthetic production of rubber has increased and new plants for synthetic textile fibres and plastics have been established—some even in the conquered countries. Production facilities for synthetic oil have been worked at full capacity and new plants have been put into operation. It would be unwise to underestimate Germany's possible achievements in this field.

Germany has been able to establish priority for her war needs and even for her civilian consumption in an efficient and regimented system that embraces the economy of the entire Continent. It has been estimated that already between one-quarter and one-sixth of her total war effort against the Allies will have been made possible by this exploitation of conquered territories.[1] Total contributions exacted under various pretexts from the occupied countries have been estimated at a minimum of £1,100,000 annually, and can be increased as Berlin may decide.

The Reich is keenly alive to the mistakes made in the last war, notably that of permitting a great decline in agricultural production. Every effort has been made to increase the labour available for agricultural purposes by employing prisoners and importing labour from occupied countries. The total number of foreign workers in Germany is more than three million. The only limit which Germany recognizes to the exploitation and regimentation of the war economy in occupied Europe is that set by the need for maintaining the economic usefulness of the conquered states. As the war continues, the bottlenecks which appeared in the German economy before the war tighten and will continue to tighten. Transportation is already overburdened as the railways system must replace sea carriers and as highway transport is hampered by the total oil situation. A growing

[1] *Economist* (April 19, 1941), p. 516.

shortage of labour is apparent in connection with the expanding substitutes industries ; and there is even some shortage in coal, which such production requires in increasing quantities.

A fuller description of Germany's supply situation after the defeat of France requires an account of imports from and through Russia. There are, of course, no official published figures. In the agreement of February 11, 1940, Russia promised to deliver oil, manganese ores, cotton, flax, phosphates, oil seeds, grain and fodder worth annually 1,100,000,000 marks.[1] We do not know to what extent this promise was kept; estimates should not be set too high. Oil delivery for 1940 was 700,000 instead of 900,000 tons, with a supply of 1,000,000 tons foreseen for 1941.[2] Equally uncertain are figures on supplies from the French colonies in North Africa—for example, those on important phosphates—and from the Near East.

On the whole, the prospects for the blockade's success over a short period changed after the conquest and exploitation of continental Europe. German experts estimate that European production can supply 90 per cent of food requirements and 93 per cent of required cereals, without, of course, any colonial products and on the basis of a strictly rationed and monotonous diet. The Institut für Konjunkturforschung[3] states for instance that crops of German Poland can be increased immediately by 20 per cent, and that the Reich can depend upon a Polish export surplus of three million tons of potatoes, which are sufficient to raise two million pigs for slaughter. The import requirement of approximately 6,700,000 tons of grain in German-occupied France, Belgium, Holland,

[1] *Deutscher Volkswirt* (February 23, 1940), pp. 658-59.
[2] *Fortune* (July 1941), p. 87.
[3] See the *Economist* (February 8, 1941), p. 183.

Denmark, and Norway can be met, it is thought, by intensifying cultivation of land for grain crops and reducing acreage used for cattle, pigs, and poultry.

The resources of the occupied countries have assured Germany a sufficient supply of iron ores, zinc, and some other commodities. Various important alloy metals are still lacking (such as chromium, nickel, tungsten, molybdenum, and vanadium), as are tin and rubber, and, of course, cotton, wool, and other textile materials. On the food side, the problem of fats will be the most serious over a longer period. The continued blockade works to produce many inconveniences and increasing difficulties, but these were less urgent than was expected as long as there have been no large active war fronts.

The most vital question connected with the effectiveness of the blockade must still be that of the Continent's supply of oil, and especially lubricating oil. The May 1941 *Bulletin* of the Petroleum Press Service publishes estimates of the annual oil requirements and supplies of Nazi Europe based upon experience since the outbreak of war. Europe's annual oil consumption before the war (without Spain and Portugal) is given as 21,300,000 tons. (Other sources say 25,000,000 tons.)[1] The *Bulletin* expresses the view that consumption, apart from military requirements, could probably be reduced to about 8,700,000 tons per annum without crippling the economic life of the countries concerned. (" Crippling " can, of course, be interpreted in different ways.) The potential annual supply at the disposal of the Nazis, including their own production of natural petroleum, coal oil, and substitute fuels, the output of Rumania (about 6,000,000 tons) and imports from Russia (about 1,000,000 tons), is estimated for the present at 11-12,000,000 tons. A margin

[1] Cf. Clarke, " Britain's Blockade," p. 13.

Economic Warfare

of about 3,000,000 tons is accordingly left for military consumption.[1]

This view seems to me over-favourable to Germany— as the statement by Frechtling also indicates. The estimated minimum need for lubricating oils is 1,100,000 tons, which is far more than the estimated maximum production in Europe. Industrial and agricultural production in continental Europe cannot be organized and maintained on a high level of efficiency without an increasing supply of oil or of various oil substitutes. Nor can the full volume of Rumanian oil be counted on (as Press Service believes) since it is known that only about a third of this can be sent via river and rail to Germany. Without accumulated oil stocks, which must be assumed to have been formed from previous conquests, Germany

---

[1] *Economist* (June 21, 1941), p. 833.

A different estimate is given by Louis E. Frechtling in "Oil and the War", p. 76. He puts Germany's requirements at approximately 55,000,000 barrels. This is exactly covered by western European production of synthetic and crude oils amounting to 37,000,000 barrels and imports from Rumania and Russia totalling 17,000,000 barrels. Only 30,000,000 barrels of Rumania oil are left for Italy and the occupied territories, whose peacetime requirements exceed 80,000,000 barrels. He concludes rightly that the Nazis cannot hope to organize the continental economy successfully without additional oil resources.

The 1940 figures for production of oil and oil substitutes (including natural gasoline, synthetic gasoline from coal, benzol, alcohol, liquid gas used as motor fuel, and shale oil products) in countries under German and Italian control were as follows (in thousands of barrels):

Country	Crude petroleum	Petroleum substitutes
Germany	4,544	20,160
Austria	719	—
Czechoslovakia	119	—
France	496	3,498
Poland (German)	1,124	75
Rumania	43,231	800
Italy	57	631
Albania	1,659	—
Total	53,704	25,244
Combined total		78,948

This total corresponds closely to that of the Petroleum Press Service.

was not in a position to embark on new large-scale military operations. She might conceivably have attempted only to defend her present conquests without a new military offensive. But this would have signified to the subject peoples of Europe that the Nazi regime faced imminent defeat. Economic warfare remains a very important factor in pressing forward Germany's military decisions.

THE PRESENT SITUATION

The economic effects of a great total war tend to expand over wider and wider areas. Neutral states suffer dislocations in export and production; exports decline because of the blockade and difficulties in shipping. In distinction from the first World War, this one has seen little profiteering by neutral countries; rather, the big producers of foodstuffs and raw materials are at a loss for markets and are accumulating surpluses[1]; and the last war experiences are not an encouraging element for great expansion of industries in overseas countries.

The United States has taken economic measures which support the economic war effort of Great Britain and a closer co-operation of both countries also in this field is developing successfully. Export control was put into

[1] *Economist* (November 9, 1940), p. 582, published the following table giving Continental Europe's imports as a percentage of non-European exports:

Wheat	32·5	Soya beans	51·8
Rye	90·7	Palm kernels	72·3
Barley	32·9	Linseed	53·9
Oats	75·0	Tobacco	43·3
Maize	45·6	Cotton	46·8
Rice	16·7	Jute	54·6
Sugar	11·2	Hemp	20·7
Cocoa	38·9	Wool	54·0
Tea	6·4	Rubber	25·1
Coffee	41·8	Oil	33·0

These figures, except for that on oil, are secured from the International Institute of Agriculture. They indicate in effect the markets lost to producers of foodstuffs and raw materials.

effect on July 2, 1940, and now covers all the important ferro-alloys, steel scrap, aluminium, magnesium, practically all other non-ferrous metals, machine tools, aircraft, and aircraft engines, equipment for production of aviation motor fuel, all arms and munitions, and many other articles. The control aims at once to maintain adequate defence supplies for the United States and to assist Great Britain and her allies by direct supply and by preventing shipment to Axis countries. The freezing of the funds of Germany and Italy and the conquered countries is another contribution to the British economic war policy. Various measures have also been taken by the United States to forestall the establishment and penetration of economic power by Germany in South America. Most important of all, the Lend-Lease Act clearly aligned the American economy with the British cause. For it made efficient aid possible by eliminating the complicated payment problems which a total war of such proportions tends to engender. The needs of a great country involved in total war must be met, not by credit, but by direct assistance.

Total war's dimensions and intensity require of the belligerent countries a progressive mobilization of all resources to meet war requirements, and, at the same time, the employment of all possible means to weaken and destroy the economic strength of the enemy. Seen in these terms Germany's position was up to the beginning of the Russian war still superior. Her basic preparation has been more complete, her arms establishment is larger, her war production is still increasing, and she is spending about 60 per cent of her national income for war purposes. If we add to these advantages all the resources she can exploit from continental Europe, we reach a figure for total war production and available productive capacity which surpasses that of the whole British Empire. On the other hand, the structure is weak at certain important points. The labour shortage will increase steadily and the transport bottlenecks consequent on closing of the sea lanes will become more menacing ; railway transport cannot replace sea transport in Europe. The whole economy is working under the severe strain of complete regimentation, and the help of the rest of the Continent is obtained only by force. It is obvious that in this situation and under the increasing pressure of blockade Germany continues to try to bring the conflict to a direct military issue—to reach a military decision after conquest in occupied territories of the Continent has helped her wage a longer war.

Great Britain has also achieved full mobilization of her economy and is spending about 50 per cent of her national income for war purposes. Canada and Australia are contributing about 30-40 per cent of their national income, and the rest of the British Commonwealth is assuming a share of the war burden. Britain has also the decisive help of the United States. She enjoys the advantages of unlimited resources of raw materials, a greater flexibility in her economic system, and her ability to count upon voluntary rather than enforced co-operation. *More and more the conflict becomes a struggle between the industry of the Nazi-dominated European continent and the industry of the British Empire and the United States ; and the industrial potential of the United States will play the decisive role.* The major influence will be exerted by the amount and efficiency of industrial capacity, the quantity and quality of the available labour force, and the size of the national income and of available reserves. Britain, indeed, faces particular difficulties : one is to cut down Germany's very considerable head start ; another is to maintain adequate shipping tonnage. What was said after the last war remains valid : " Behind all the elaborate mechanism of economic warfare the paramount importance of control of the seas both as a means of defence for Great Britain and as an instrument of attack stands out as a simple fact."[1] She must as far as necessary and possible prevent a recurrence of the last war's experience, when the volume of imports to Great Britain declined from 55,000,000 tons in 1913 to 46,000,000 tons in 1916 and to only 35,000,000 tons in 1918.[2] The task of the British Navy and Marine is much greater in the present war. If these difficulties can be overcome—and there is reason to expect that they will—then Great Britain's chance is really greater in the long run. To an economy dictatorially governed and based on forced labour, mechanized to complete inflexibility, without internal reserves and subject to complete blockade, she can oppose an efficient mobilization of practically unlimited economic resources and very great productive capacities, operating democratically and with a maximum flexibility. The importance of the economic aid of the United States is clearly vital. If to the economic pressure effective military and moral pressure is added, a break may well be effected in the over-strained German system. And such is the tension of the entire overcharged structure that the collapse of the whole may very rapidly follow.

What effects may be expected from the German-Russian war, in which Germany certainly hopes to secure new supplies of oil, food, minerals, and various raw materials for the long war which she now anticipates? The blockade is now absolutely effective for the first time: supplies from Russia to Germany and other European

---

[1] D. T. Jack, *Studies in Economic Warfare*, p. 145.

[2] *Ibid*, p. 117. The shipping losses of Great Britain and her allies reached in June 1941 the figure of more than 7,000,000 tons or nearly 5 per cent of known available shipping space.

countries are at an end. Huge amounts of war materials of all kinds, especially of precious oil, are being consumed. If Russia can resist for a protracted period, Germany's supply of oil and perhaps some other materials may be seriously depleted. If Germany defeats Russia quickly and occupies the Ukraine and Caucasus regions, she must still execute the difficult task of organizing the Russian economy so as to extract from it the required supplies. Quite apart from the destruction of plants which the Russians are expected to carry out, the task will take a long time. The Russian economy, which is now mechanized in both agriculture and industry, has required progressively more oil, which has been difficult to supply out of the Russian production. The whole system is interrelated (Soviet farm machinery uses about 6,000,000 tons of petrol annually with a tendency toward increase) and not susceptible of an easy transformation. Germany could obtain oil or grain but not both. If Germany can effect this reorganization, her economic and military position will indeed be very strong —although she will still be without sufficient supplies of important commodities like rubber, nickel, tin, molybdenum, tungsten, wool—and the stalemate feared before the Russian war began will again become a possibility. Time would then favour Germany, although she would face an even greater labour shortage, difficulty in transport, and over all passive resistance. It is therefore most important for Great Britain not to allow Germany to consolidate her position in Europe by overcoming and absorbing the Russian economy. The Allies, including the United States, must speed up war production in all fields. Success in this effort is the first and most vital step towards the final decision.

CHAPTER V

FROM WAR TO PEACE

THE WAR AND THE WORLD ECONOMY

THE economic impact of total war is felt as soon as the war begins and widens steadily until the whole world is affected, directly or indirectly. The combatants mobilize all the economic resources available : all energy, all work is devoted to the one purpose of carrying on the war. In the present struggle, the free economy aimed at welfare will be progressively abandoned in region after region in favour of war economy. The countries that have remained neutral in Europe are themselves living under the strain of war, spending vast amounts on national defence and severely regimenting their national economies. Overseas neutrals are suffering from dislocation of their foreign trade as stocks of food and raw materials pile up ; the strain on public finances steadily increases. In a total war between great countries, one of which is a totalitarian regime of the Nazi type, neutrality in the old sense is meaningless and there is no real escape from the effects of war.[1]

The nature and progress of the conflict demonstrates now very plainly the impossibility of co-operation, even in the economic sphere, between the democratic and the Nazi regimes. This should have been seen long ago. The development of the Russian system disrupted the

---

[1] *Economist* (April 19, 1941), p. 529 : " Never in previous wars have neutrality virtues been so poorly rewarded as they are at present, with the trade of the world utterly disorganized, materials piling up in producing countries and prevented by blockade and counter-blockade from reaching their normal markets."

European balance and was very harmful to international economic co-operation. But the Russian part in the continental economy was somewhat different from the German. Russia was before 1917 largely pre-capitalistic, engaged in a very small proportion of foreign trade, and not closely related to the world economy. Later, Communist Russia's foreign trade operated openly through state agencies and in a limited number of commodities, so that its influence on the world market was far less than that of the organized German trading drive under the Nazi regime.

Despite general knowledge of Nazi methods and the immediately unpleasant experience suffered by international business in dealing with post-war Germany, the latter's policy of economic aggression was in the main met by economic appeasement—prior to and co-incident with the phase of actual political appeasement. Analysis reveals a great variety of motives behind this appeasement. Side by side with a naïve pacifism there existed a comprehensible fear of the destructive impact of a new war; of considerable weight, too, were the fears of bolshevism and of social changes, as well as internal differences within nations aroused by differing attitudes toward the economic *status quo*; while vested interests influenced also the attitude of various important groups, and there was much materialism, egoism, opportunism. All these were exploited in masterly fashion to further the Nazi effort.

The nations lacked solidarity, both within themselves and in their dealings with one another. Only by shutting their eyes to the violation of international understandings and basic human rights could the leaders of the democracies maintain their dealings with the Nazis on the established economic basis. They believed that they could do business with this new system and yet preserve untouched and aloof their own ideas, interests, and spheres of activity. They failed to recognize the basic nature of the whole conflict. Thus there is considerable reason to call the present war not only a conflict between nations but also a civil war, supported and used by Germany and affecting most nations internally. The existence and usefulness to the Nazis of this conflict was shown very clearly in the fall of France. To appease the Nazis and refuse to see the problem as it really was offered no solution; the alternatives were, clearly, to yield or to oppose, which meant, eventually, to fight.

It is, of course, still too early to speak of the economic consequences of the war. We do not know yet its extent or intensity or duration. But some developments are certain: the power of the state over economic life has increased everywhere; free economy has been replaced by war economy throughout the world, with correlative features of dislocation and control; the fabric of international trade and world markets has been severely torn; as a whole Europe's position relative to other continents has been weakened; the weakness of the smaller states in the existing international order has been clearly demonstrated; enormous proportions of national production and income have been devoted to one destructive purpose while the level of living in much of the world has declined and public debts have everywhere risen to hitherto unknown proportions.

The war does not and cannot settle the fundamental problems. Its effects will tend rather to aggravate them. But it can perhaps bring some of them to a sharper focus and thus render their character more clear.

The fundamental task is still to develop a new economic equilibrium in the world and to restore a social balance within the nations. Essentially connected with this is the establishment of a new constitution, political and economic, for the countries taken severally and together. There has been urgent need for this for the past twenty-five years; now it must be carried out, not only in the face of the economic and social effects of the present war but also in spite of a universal destruction of confidence and disrespect of law and decency and all human rights, positive and inherent. The task is without question far more difficult than it would have been in 1930 or 1931. Whether its fulfilment will take a democratic or a totalitarian form depends, of course, on the outcome of the war.

THE TOTALITARIAN PLAN FOR THE "NEW ORDER"

Germany has, of course, a blueprint for the so-called "new economic and political order" in Europe and the world. Although all details have not been elaborated and the plan changes from time to time, its essential features are delineated in sufficient clarity to show how the Reich expects to proceed.[1]

The theory fundamental to this blueprint for a new German Empire—which will certainly include the European continent with the Ukraine and oil-producing territories of Russia and some areas of Asia and Africa—is that of the necessity of large-scale economic units, of *Grossraumwirtschaft*. Europe will be organized into one economic unit directed by Germany; politically there are various possibilities involving protectorates, vassal states, pseudo-independent states, and others. The economy of this unit will continue to function on the basis established during the war. It will become independent

---

[1] Among the official statements are the well-known speech of Dr Funk, Reichsminister of Economics, on July 25, 1940, and a special annex to *Deutscher Volkswirt* on December 20, 1940, which contains, among others, articles by high officials like Helmuth Wohltat, Carl Ritter, and Emil Puhl, as well as essays and statements on special problems.

of the outside world in respect of foodstuffs and indispensable industrial materials.[1] And in large measure it will be freed from dependence on the world market and from the influence of world business cycles. It has to guarantee to Germany a maximum of economic security and a maximum also of goods consumption. This is the goal of the new European economy ruled by Germany.

The Nazis argue that only on the assured basis of a United Europe can really fruitful exchange be developed in foodstuffs, raw materials, and industrial goods. Central control of the continental economy must therefore continue. Unemployment must be eliminated; financial and credit policy is to be regulated with that aim in view. In the attainment of autarchy it will be necessary to bring all agriculture up to the German level, guaranteeing higher prices for agricultural products: the German sacrifice which this may entail will be balanced by the increased prosperity in central and eastern Europe.

Berlin is to acquire property or control in all key industries and important factories on the Continent, especially in iron and coal industries, the chemical industry, munitions production, and the railway systems. European production in agriculture as well as industry is to be redistributed; even population is to be transferred according to its density[2] and to the supply of food in the

---

[1] See Erich Neumann, Secretary of State in the Ministry of Economics, in the *German-American Commerce Bulletin* (March 1941), p. 12; and Helmuth Wohltat, in *Deutscher Volkswirt* (December 20, 1940), p. 958.

[2] The following figures are taken from the Nazi blueprint as presented by Paul Wohl in the *Providence Journal* (May 4, 1941), p. 2. Greater Germany with a population of 86,200,000 can feed only 74,100,000; 12,100,000 must find " living space " elsewhere. Italy must find space for 3,100,000 of these, Holland for 4,900,000, and Belgium for 5,000,000. On the other hand, according to Nazi estimates, France may be racially exploited by Nazi methods so as to absorb 23,100,000 Germans and Italians —Spain 27,200,000. There will, furthermore, be plenty of space in eastern and south-eastern Europe: according to the blueprint, Poland could feed, beyond her present population, 18,300,000, Hungary 8,000,000,

various countries. The non-German sections will preferably be built up as suppliers of food and raw materials for Greater Germany, where the most important industrial production is to be located. The process of industrialization in non-German areas will be stopped.

Labour will be saved by the improvement of manufacturing techniques, and the level of living will be raised by the universal establishment of mass production. Prices will be unaffected by those of other continents; the profit motive will cease to be respected as an important factor; the entire Continent will be managed as was the German war economy. A clear distinction will be maintained among the various nations and races in accordance with the German conception of racial superiority, with the German master race ruling the whole. In such a system there will, of course, be no free foreign trade or foreign exchange, as this must be integrated into the total economic system. Prices and wages will be subject to control, with the price system organized for the Continent as a unit.

The reichsmark is to become the dominant monetary unit, with the economy in general being governed by a " mark standard ". So far as other currencies remain, they will be pegged to the mark on an officially stated basis. Berlin will replace London as a financial centre,

---

Rumania 19,100,000, and Yugoslavia 10,200,000; this depends, of course, on replacing the out-moded routine of traditional economy with Nazi efficiency. Were the Nazi genius for organization given a free hand it could produce enough in Russia to feed 600,000,000 more than the present population.

Another statement by Professor Ernst Wagemann, director of the Berlin Institute for Business Research, appeared in the German press on August 13, 1941. According to it the continent of Europe without Russia should be able to provide sufficient food from its own agricultural production for the feeding of the population of 460,000,000, while at present a population of only 343,000,000 is dependent for 9 per cent of its total food requirements on imports from other countries. New York *Times*, August 14, 1941, p. 8.

and Germany will become the creditor nation of Europe, using the contributions and assets secured by her conquests to establish this position. Intra-continental trade will operate on the basis of multilateral clearing agreements which are considered the most appropriate instrument for encouraging and ordering such trade. By this device national economies will be enabled to follow a price and credit policy not directly affected by international markets. There will be great flexibility in the price policy; the whole system will develop a balanced and stable condition in prices as well as in goods within the clearing community.[1] Economic development in general will be greatly facilitated, and the economy will be manipulated very efficiently by fixing the rate of exchange. The Nazi order will, of course, be internally independent of gold; no " gold is behind the Mark, which is supported only by the industry of the German worker ", says an official statement. The only usefulness gold may enjoy is in the settling of international balances. But we find also the statement that some day it may be discovered that a storage of coal is a better reserve for settlements than is the overflooded accumulation of the United States Treasury.

As a whole this new German economic empire, whose population will be at least 325,000,000, can be compared with an enormous economic trust, owned and centrally controlled by Berlin. The German people will be specially privileged, with the rest of Europe subordinated and adjusted as German needs require. The "new order" is already being put into effect[2] and extended as

[1] "Kreditgeschaft und multilateraler Verrechnungsverkehr," by H. H. H. Hohlfeld, *Deutsche Volkswirtschaft* (1940), No. 25, p. 766.

[2] See Louis Domeratzky, "Germany's Plans for Post-War Economy: Their Scope and Implications," *Foreign Commerce Weekly* (May 10, 1941), and Antonín Basch, "The New Order in Europe—An Accomplished Fact," *Free World*, No. 1, New York, October, 1941.

far as conditions of war permit. At the same time, the process of conquest is an instrument most apt for the achievement of this central aim. There are various important steps in the German effort to bring this " new order " into being. In the realm of territorial settlement, Austria, Bohemia and Moravia, western Poland, Alsace-Lorraine, and Luxemburg have been directly incorporated into Greater Germany. It does not, indeed, make any great economic difference whether a country is thus incorporated or is one of the occupied countries, or even a unit like unoccupied France or one of the remaining neutrals (though here the difference is greater), since on all of these the pressure of the German economy (and the dependence on it) is increasingly heavy. As has been explained in the previous chapter, the system of multilateral clearing agreements was introduced to enable Germany to exploit the European continent as her needs require. In practice, the German mark has been established as the continental standard, governing all currencies pegged to it and thereby regulating the price levels in various countries. By simply changing the exchange rate between the mark and other currencies, Germany can buy at lower prices and require other countries to pay higher prices—in other words, she can get more foreign goods and more foreign labour for less German goods and German labour. Even neutrals like Sweden and Switzerland have been brought into this system. The principles of the German war economy are all-embracing, affecting alike the regimentation of prices and wages and the adjustment of production and rationing of consumption. Customs barriers are adjusted or even wholly abolished to fit the German economic programme. As the war goes on, Germany aims to establish complete control over European industry and banking. She is therefore making strenuous efforts to achieve, by seemingly legal means, an interest in the most important enterprises. Various devices are employed to secure property belonging to conquered states—factories, banks, forests, farms, and shipping companies. Some have been seized outright, others put under German management. The procedure of " Aryanization " (taking property from people considered non-Aryans in the German definition) has been followed in all countries in order to transfer important properties to German hands without any real compensation or countervalue. Heavy pressure has been used in many cases under other pretexts of various kinds, as in acquiring French property in the Balkans. Payments have generally been made out of contributions extracted from those countries as war indemnity or for some other reason : a country would in effect reduce its war reparations by surrendering its most important industrial and banking establishments. Thus a system of looting concealed by various legal pretences and titles is being used to pave the way for the German economic empire in Europe. Already the Germans have gained ownership or control of the most important industries and banks as well as of the whole monetary system ; they are trying by every means to establish this " New Order ", in order to present it as an accomplished fact.

The question is, What does this " new order " mean from the point of view of a permanent solution? It does not represent an organic or integrated agreement expressing the co-operation of nations ; it does not respect basic human rights. It claims to supply two important needs of the present system : the formation of a large economic unit that will make possible rationalized mass production and consumption, and economic security for all in the form of an assured occupation.

The plan does not, of course, restore world political and economic balance or lay a foundation for peace. On the contrary, it makes for continued war inside Europe and outside as well. It projects a Europe self-sufficient as far as possible, bargaining as one mighty unit with other regions. Its premise is thus that Europe can be so transformed as to form an autarchic entity. But the picture of European trade in 1937, or in any previous year when international economic co-operation was proceeding at a moderate pace, shows this premise to be false. It indicates clearly that Europe does not possess any real means of becoming a prosperous self-sufficient economy. To make this possible, parts of Russia, Africa, and Asia must be included. Even then, its success will depend upon Germany's having time to organize and develop the whole economy, upon the extent of *ersatz* (substitutes) production, upon the standard of living which the nations will be both able to accept and willing to continue, upon Germany's political ability to compel the states to co-operate—taking into account the whole policing system, and upon the responsiveness of other parts of the world in co-operating with a Europe dominated by the Nazis.

It is certainly impossible to provide Europe, by domestic quantity production, with tropical products like coffee, cotton, cocoa, natural rubber, various fruits, and other colonial products. Nor are minerals such as tin and nickel available in Europe in any considerable quantity. But the figures for 1937 or for previous years cannot be used as a final basis since they represent the old " static " in contrast with the intended new " dynamic " order. There is no doubt that a certain increase in self-sufficiency can be achieved by local transfer of industry, by intensifying agriculture, by further extending production of substitutes, and by more closely regulating consumption, particularly if the important Russian areas are included. But this would involve a lowered standard of living : on the whole the European nations would receive far less for their work than they had in the period of free international co-operation.

The large German economic unit would, of course, be very powerful in bargaining in international trade, especially as it dealt with the smaller countries producing foodstuffs and raw materials that had previously been exported in great quantities to Europe and for which no other markets are available. The attempt would be made to impose trading terms upon all these smaller or weaker nations—that is, to repeat, especially in South America, the same policy of economic penetration which was pursued successfully in central and eastern Europe. As it was there impossible to deal on equal terms with Germany and at the same time preserve a free system of trade, so it would be impossible in dealings with a German-dominated Europe to maintain private and unregulated trade. In place of international co-operation we should set the growth of economic control in areas hitherto free, and economic warfare would continue in even sharper degree. The trend is manifest in the blacklisting by the United States on July 17, 1941, of certain firms in Central and South America : Americans are forbidden to trade with any firm on this list, in view of the affiliation with the interests of Germany or of countries dominated by her. This is a step in preventing Germany from securing in Central and South America footholds which would permit her in the future to continue the policy of economic penetration with all its ramifications.

As knowledge of German trading methods is spread abroad, the opinion that free foreign trade for America is compatible with satisfactory dealings with a victorious Germany is held by fewer and fewer people : the number so minded is an increasingly slight minority. There is now a more or less general conviction that, should Germany win the war, even an economic unit as powerful as the United States would be able to trade with her only if measures of control were taken to defend American interests.[1] There are some optimists who do not believe that Germany can succeed in organizing Europe to a higher degree of self-sufficiency and that, in the end, overwhelming economic resources and a sounder economic policy must win out. They are satisfied that a victorious Germany will spontaneously change her system or be forced to change in due course of time. But anyone who knows the thorough consistency of the Nazi system will dismiss from consideration the possibility of a voluntary change : no permanent change in foreign trade or general economic policy is to be expected. It is possible that a change might be forced upon the Nazis by structural weaknesses or by their inability to police and govern the subject peoples. But to rely upon that possibility is to disregard the damage and suffering attendant upon the experiment involved in such a regime. We have seen already what the Nazis have done to the world and to the world economy in eight years. No one can even guess the extent of loss and destruction if the continent of Europe remains for a longer time under an economy so disturbing to the whole world and so likely to destroy the most important fundaments of future reconstruction.

There is no real or permanent solution in Hitler's "new order". It achieves only the fulfilment of Germany's desire to dominate ; its origins and motives are purely materialistic, in spite of the Nazi condemnation of " materialistic " capitalism. There is no higher idea in it than German advancement. It sees no freedom of

---

[1] See also Douglas Miller, *You Can't Do Business with Hitler*. Little, Brown & Company, Boston, 1941.

nations but only a primitive sort of autonomy. It guarantees no freedom of individuals, no assurance of basic human rights. Instead, it offers economic advantages within the managed German *Grossraumwirtschaft* in Europe, and a type of economic security and social justice promised to labour in return for the renunciation of freedom and essential rights. But even the most ingenious propaganda cannot prove that labour, by working in this German Empire trust, without freedom and with economic considerations subordinated to politics, will receive more than in a free world based on an international exchange of commodities and following fundamental economic principles.

THE DEMOCRATIC PROGRAMME

In opposing Germany's plan for a European *Grossraumwirtschaft* dominated by Germany and offering a type of economic security and social justice in place of the basic rights of free society, the democratic powers must work out a constructive platform which conforms to the real possibilities of the world economy and combines freedom, both of nations and individuals, with an improved economic organization in which the promise of social justice is more substantial. The task is not easy, but the democracies can call upon vast resources, political, economic, and social. It need not be pointed out that world economic resources are ample, that the basic problem is one of international economic organization, of transforming the technical possibilities of production so as to satisfy human needs.

We must never forget this fundamental fact—there can be in the present world economy no satisfactory and lasting order which rests upon gross differences in levels of living among nations and within nations whose economies are highly developed. The war has shown the inherent solidarity of the world economy, whether this is openly admitted or not.

The crisis consequent on the technological revolution after the first World War and aggravated by the contracting effects of autarchic economic policies on both world and national economies is reminiscent—although its intensities and scope is obviously far greater—of the social crisis in the first half of the nineteenth century. That crisis was connected with the first technological revolution and was overcome only by an economic policy which encouraged the expansion of production and consumption, both nationally and internationally. Such a policy of expansion is the only solution of the present crisis—it must be taken up and promoted as our essential creed, our guiding idea.

THE PROBLEM OF ECONOMIC DEMOCRACY AND SECURITY

It is not my intention here to discuss the whole post-war reconstruction which will require a very detailed study. I shall mention only two important phases, connected especially with Europe. These are the much discussed topics of economic democracy and the formation of a United States of Europe—the first a problem in national economic control and unemployment, the other the problem of determining the position of the small states and the general reorganization of Europe.

The problem of economic democracy and national economic control, long the subject of fundamental discussions, became acutely real when the world was confronted with the greatest unemployment of modern times, a total of thirty million unemployed. This unemployment afforded the Nazis a very important weapon in their propaganda for a promised new order which would wipe out the plutocratic corruption of existing capitalism. And the task of a modern state is very often conceived as that of assuring full utilization of its human and material resources and maintaining a national income of adequate dimensions. The question is whether this demand can be satisfied in a democratic system—further, whether such a demand is justified in a democratic society and how far the society may go in answering it while maintaining its democratic basis.

Clearly we must first determine what we shall include under the notion of a democratic regime. Every definition changes with time, save for its most essential elements. What then is essential for democracy? We know it is not a form of government, not a definite system for holding elections. Rather, it is the principle of freedom, of respect for and assurance of basic human rights, including certain principles of economic organization. I think that the content of modern democracy was extremely well formulated by President Roosevelt, who gave as its essentials freedom of speech, of press, and of religion, freedom from want, and from fear.[1] I do not accept the identification of democracy with the economic system of liberal capitalism; nor do I believe that democracy will necessarily give way to a totalitarian regime if economic life is subjected to a certain form of central control or planning. But equally I refuse to believe that it is possible to retain democracy and freedom together with a totalitarian management of the economic system, except, of course, in emergency or war.

Those who oppose state interference and favour the automatic working of economic forces overlook the fact that a modern national economy is subject to such controls, of private and public varieties, that the free play of automatic forces has very largely disappeared. The

---

[1] A. D. Lindsay is quoted in the *Economist* (December 28, 1940), p. 789, as saying (in his *I Believe in Democracy*) that " the aim and purpose of all governments ought to be to increase freedom, to encourage and protect all the free voluntary activities of men and women in society ".

control is not developed by the state alone : within the sphere of private economy there has been built up a system of administration which has worked to establish prices with increasing inflexibility. One could speak, in many countries, of privately administered wages and prices. Large concentrations of industrial production, due to technical development, have created over and above natural or technical monopolies a trend toward economic monopoly. The industrial agreements involved in mass production brought with them a decline in efficient competition ; complexities developed in the adjustment of production, prices, and wages. And when, under the impact of the world crisis, private economy proved unable to cope with the emergency as quickly as was necessary, it was in fact the development of rigidity within private industry rather than the often assailed state interference that delayed the process of re-adjustment. It was truly said that " Individual action cannot plan security for all or control the trade cycles ".[1]

In the great crisis of " scarcity in the midst of plenty ", there was much opposition in European countries between the advocates of extensive planning and the defenders of free economy. It became clear that the normal administration in a parliamentary democracy was neither able nor equipped to meet the situation. Nor could either of the basic economic groups exercise the proper control—capital, though still an important factor in economic life, was without direct political influence, and labour had neither direct representation nor responsibility in the direction of economic life. That period in which the state tried to attack the economic crisis by an active business cycle policy was far from happy. On all sides it was urged that direction of economic matters be taken out of politics and placed in the hands of

[1] *Economist* (December 28, 1940), p. 790.

independent agencies; experience had shown that political parties tried to impose their particular interests upon the administration in specific economic decisions. The combination of administrative complexity and party interest was thought insurmountable, and the fear grew steadily that planning of a political type would not solve the vital problems of production, trade, and employment. It was predicted that such planning, if extended to the more important sectors of economic and social life, would, rather, become authoritarian and end in the complete suppression of freedom. I think that the experience of the democracies during the past decade in extensive planning and managing of national economy may provide a very good basis for determining the limits and methods for democratic control and planning in general.

Germany, of course, solved the problem of unemployment in totalitarian fashion by putting her entire economy on a war basis in time of peace and by introducing, in later stages, the extreme expedient of compulsory labour. It is obvious that if there is one practically unlimited goal for the system of production, full production will be carried on—as is the normal condition in total war. But I do not accept the conclusion that the war economy demonstrates the possibility of achieving full employment by direct government management of production and consumption or that the new system of direct economic management has settled the difficult question of the proper ratio between consumption and investment by giving the government absolute control over the economic machine.[1]

Although there may be a post-war period of reconstruction during which the government will direct great segments of national production (as the building activity

---

[1] See Peter F. Drucker, "Must a War Economy Be Permanent?" in *Harper's Magazine* (May, 1941), pp. 569-77.

in Great Britain), I doubt whether such commandeering can continue permanently in peacetime within a democratic regime. It is only in the face of tasks of wartime dimensions that a democracy can assign such powers to government. We know of such comprehensive planning and of determination by government of the ratio between consumption and investment—in Russia. But how could such complete management of production be harmonized with freedom of initiative and enterprise and with freedom of occupation? And in addition to this primary problem how could a comprehensive blueprint be worked out for the whole complicated machine of modern industry, whose productive activities are now so highly concentrated? A dynamic life would be governed and hampered by a static administration. The example of government interference in many European countries is not encouraging; administration has become vastly complex and an increased amount of unproductive effort has been expended in public as well as in private life. It is obvious that such an enormous concentration of economic power would entail undesirable political consequences, more serious in fact than the difficulties which the government has been assigned to remove. The problem needs a thorough analysis in its most basic terms and in the light of the experience of the past decade. In my opinion, Henry M. Wriston is entirely correct in saying "Economic dictatorship does not and indeed cannot stop with economic matters. If political power can commandeer productive energies it may, indeed it must, control all energies."[1] It is unrealistic to imagine that political control based on general elections can be of itself effective.

To meet the demand upon them the democracies must

[1] Henry M. Wriston, *Prepare for Peace* (Harper & Brothers, New York, 1941), p. 256.

elaborate some plan at once feasible and in line with their evolution. It is obvious that the problem of mass employment, including the problem of youth, must be attacked and organically solved. But very general problems arise : if we acknowledge as our basic principle that everyone has a right to a job, we must assert a corresponding duty to accept what jobs are offered—freedom must be weighed against control, and so on.

The democratic answer to the basic offer of political and economic order must be : order and wealth, order and liberty.[1] The problem is the object of active discussion in Great Britain, and it is very significant that the discussion proceeds from the basis of a sound progressive evolution which attempts to graft the new upon the old.[2] Thus discussion of the problem comes to examination of the ultimate limits of economic planning within a democratic regime. The general principle may be asserted that these limits are found at the point where it becomes impossible or extremely difficult to reach the agreement which forms a basis for the policy of the democratic state. As a rule, an active business-cycles policy attended by a certain degree of planning has been accepted as falling within the limits of the modern state's economic power. Associated with this has been monetary and credit policy and public finance. The conception of this last has, indeed, undergone profound changes during the last ten or fifteen years, as it has become understood that production is the essential problem and finance technical and secondary to it (however difficult it may be

[1] British Foreign Secretary Anthony Eden in his speech on May 29, 1941.

[2] In this connection see also Eduard Beneš, *Democracy Today and Tomorrow* (Macmillan, London, 1939), Harold Laski, *Where Do We Go From Here?* (Penguins, London, 1940), Francis Williams, *War by Revolution* (Routledge, London, 1940), and *Programme for Victory*, by Laski, Nicolson, Cole, and others (Routledge, London, 1941).

in fact to provide the appropriate financial organization).[1] A general interference with actual and potential monopolies is also recognized and favoured, although this policy must be so shaped as not to prevent new technical developments, which themselves act to fight and break down monopolies. It is in the nature of technical production that large-scale concentrations are constantly broken down by the establishment of new small plants. And finally, a comprehensive system of social security is acknowledged to be essential to modern governmental activity. The question of what kinds of enterprise are to be subject to direct state control or property is not, of course, exactly the same for all states; the answer must vary according to historical and local factors. In general, the less developed and industrialized the national economy, the less the state interference that is regarded as necessary and useful.

All the above-mentioned measures of state economic policy are alike in that they lie in the field of general planning. They do not enter the region of detailed planning in which a democracy is bound to encounter real difficulties. They involve, at most, general directions or general prohibitions issued by government, applying equally to all persons. When on the other hand government attempts to determine and administer detailed matters of production, consumption, or trade, it finds itself without any real basis for a proper decision, without what F. von Hayek calls " the detailed code of values ". In that case there is great danger of arbitrary decisions and a tendency to expand planning to new spheres on the theory that its success depends upon its completeness and comprehensiveness.

[1] G. D. H. Cole says, in *Programme for Victory*, p. 104 : " We shall have to base incomes on what we can produce, instead of limiting production to what incomes can buy."

I believe that if the state limits its interference to general control (that is, mainly to the problem of business cycles and of unemployment), the major part of economic life can remain unregulated and unmanaged, except as direction follows naturally from the play of private enterprise and free initiative. This negotiated free economy can again be developed in a dynamic fashion and can, as a general expanding tendency is resumed, dispose of the structural bottleneck of technological unemployment more quickly than could an extensive overall planning. And such a negotiated, disciplined free economy will more readily conduce to a new social equilibrium in which labour finds its proper status, capital is accorded its appropriate influence upon political life, and the profit motive is sufficiently co-ordinated to harmonize with the demands of the general welfare.

RECONSTRUCTION OF EUROPE

For the reconstruction of Europe the formation of the United States of Europe as one large economic unit has been frequently proposed. But such a unit, regardless of its immediate utility or its likelihood in the near future, does not constitute a solution of Europe's position in the world economy. As I have already pointed out, Europe is, as a whole, dependent upon the import of food and raw materials from other territories. This situation is not met by the creation of a European unit, unless a policy of self-sufficiency, with its attendant decline in the standard of living, is to be maintained.

The position of Europe is determined by her structure, population, and traditions, all of which are adjusted to exchanging manufactured goods and services for raw materials, foodstuffs, and other goods. The interests of the world economy require that she continue in this rôle;

and only in a revival of economic expansion on a world basis can a real solution for Europe be worked out.

We here encounter, it is true, various objections centring about the theory of the declining importance of foreign trade and the related theory of economic maturity which some countries at present are thought to have attained. Both of these emphasize only static elements: they resemble the conception of the totally planned economy in not granting sufficient weight to the dynamic and flexible aspects of the European economy. The theory of maturity, in its assertion that there is no more free land to be cultivated, that the greatest technical achievements have already been performed, the largest investments already made, and in its conclusion that any further development must be very slow, is directly at odds with the policy of international co-operation, of mutual stimulation, of encouraging the ever fresh energies of free initiative: it offers only an isolationist and static economic view. The state of maturity which it describes cannot be regarded as the necessary result of the structure of the national economies but only as the outcome of a temporary and isolated bottleneck situation, which has arisen from a particular national and international economic policy.

The theory of the declining importance of foreign trade was much influenced by the German doctrine underlying the policy of self-sufficiency. This doctrine urges the procedure of completing the national economy as the proper basis for foreign trade, with deliberate restrictions upon exchange of commodities, instead of permitting foreign trade and the national economy to develop, as experience has shown they will, by their mutual interplay. As a national economy reaches a higher stage of general economic activity, the new needs that are created stimulate equally production and consumption; in such an expansion the impact of free initiative results in a foreign trade of corresponding vitality. It would be over pessimistic to believe that the present world has already reached the stage of static maturity. In point of fact, this theory of declining foreign trade and of comprehensive planning with a view to a completed economy is very dangerous. Control of foreign trade, as the experience of the last decades teaches us, is always under pressure to admit only goods considered necessary to the importing nation. It is certain to reflect the influence of competitors and in general its effect has been to contract the volume of international trade.[1]

The development of foreign trade is a matter not only of exporting mass products in return for the materials of backward areas. Psychological and technical shackles have been imposed during the past decades to impede trade between highly developed countries; were foreign trade liberated from these the possibilities in terms of new needs and new exchange are very great. Only in such a new expansion of foreign trade can the position of the European Continent be made secure, even though this conclusion requires discarding many notions of recent years and returning to examination of the essential features of Europe's place in world economy. Co-operation with other continents, and especially with the British Commonwealth and the United States, is fundamental to any further progress in Europe, and so, in part, to the world economy at large.

When I say that the United States of Europe does not in itself offer a solution to the real problem, I do not intend to advocate a return to the *status quo* of before

[1] " When the political authority becomes the principal in international trade the motivating force in that trade ceases to be economy; it takes its nature from the State and becomes political." Wriston, *Prepare for Peace*, p. 94.

the outbreak of war. The war economy now maintained by Germany will, of course, dislocate production severely and, further, will create many ultimately unproductive facilities, which can be carried on only at a great waste of both labour and capital. But it may exert in some measure an integrating influence, both psychological and economic, on the European reconstruction. It is quite possible that such integrating influence will be effective in levelling prices and the cost of production and also in the monetary system. The elimination of different levels in production and in the independent monetary units may well facilitate, later on, the formation of larger economic units.

The problem of the small states in Europe is, of course, very important. The system of collective security failed, and confidence in a new system of similar nature will not be easily developed. The war showed very plainly the economic, political, and military weakness of the small states in a total war with a great power ; this experience may be the most compelling reason for a closer association of the smaller states. On the other hand, the demand for larger economic units will become less intense as international exchange of commodities returns to a more liberal basis and counteracts the centralizing tendency inherent in the technical character of present industrial production. The problem is more pressing in central and eastern Europe than in the West. A first step has already been taken in the form of an agreement between the Czechoslovak and Polish governments concluded in November 1940, looking to a close co-operation in the political as well as the economic field ; the precise form has yet to be worked out. It is expected that other nations in this part of Europe will join in this basic agreement, and we may hope that the bitter experience of recent years may help to diminish the exaggerated nationalism which has done so much damage in the economic as well as the political field.

When we ask what type of unit may be best for these states, we must reply in terms of a certain similarity of economic and social structure and a basic conformity in political ideas. The same considerations will determine its form—whether customs union, or a closer economic unit with a common or adjusted monetary system, and so on. Without a detailed analysis, it appears that an economic group might be formed including Austria, Czechoslovakia, Hungary, Poland, Rumania, and Yugoslavia, assuming changes in the political and social structure of Hungary and Rumania, and of Poland in some degree. Such a group would muster a population of about a hundred million and could present a strong economic front. The addition of Switzerland would strengthen it considerably. What is of prime importance is that no large power should be a member of such a unit. A similar unit might be formed by the so-called Oslo group containing the Scandinavian countries and The Netherlands.

The problem of agricultural export from central and eastern Europe, although very difficult during the last crisis, will not present serious complexities in the years immediately following the war, as Europe is, taken as a whole, deficient in agricultural production. Subsequently the best solution will be to increase the purchasing power of these backward areas, whose consumption of agricultural products has been abnormally low; this will automatically reduce the agricultural surplus. And if perhaps for a certain length of time it is necessary to employ preferential customs for this part of Europe, the impact on overseas trade will be slight, in view of the small quantities in the total surplus.

The problem of Germany will not be easy. Europe

obviously needs Germany, both as producer and as consumer, but German foreign relations will be very delicate. The experience of dealing with Germany, in politics as well as in economic activity, will not be forgotten—the broken promises, the friends whose business was employed in the service of the Nazis, the hatred, sowed by Germany, that has taken root. It is questionable whether people in general will accept the widely spread thesis distinguishing the Nazis from the Germans—and those who reject the thesis can hardly be blamed.

Russia offers another great problem. Co-operation between her and the rest of Europe, which was conspicuously lacking after the last war, may be of great importance to the recovery of the European economy. We may hope that out of the present military co-operation may come some kind of adjustment in the Russian economic regime, tending to restore the trend toward economic democracy which Russian communism once promised and which has been revived piecemeal since 1938. A democratic victory in the present conflict will so implement the psychological momentum of the democratic cause that Russia will not be sufficiently strong to resist the pressure of such an adjustment.

The projected economic co-operation of the smaller states will be so close as to require a certain limitation of their sovereignty; as in the national economy the process of democracy calls for some restrictions on economic liberty, so in international affairs freedom must also be subjected to some co-operative controls. Even the great powers must themselves acknowledge such controls if a new organization of the world economy is to be worked out.

It is my conviction that it would be in the interest of future European organization to have the peace treaties include such special agreements for co-operation, together with the mechanism for putting them into effect. This mechanism could be related to the various international institutions which we may expect to issue from the peace and from the new efforts at world economic reconstruction. The automatic functioning of the world economy which prevailed before 1914 must be replaced by an organized co-operation, in regard to credit and international finance, in the development of backward areas, in control of raw materials, and so on. All of this presupposes indeed a real solidarity of all the important factors in the world economy, with the United States assuming such responsibility as is appropriate to its economic and political power.

PERIOD OF TRANSITION

I cannot offer here a thorough analysis of the period of transition from war- to peace-time economy. It is probable that the experience which followed the last war will lead the nations to initiate a phase of general transition before the final settlement is made. In this phase, the administered war economy must be changed to a free disciplined peacetime economy through the effort of internationally organized and planned co-operation. Of particular concern will be elimination of the unemployment that threatens to follow the cessation of war production; this problem has already been extensively studied in Great Britain. The European nations will no doubt be very anxious to dispense with all the regimentation, all the obstacles to trade under which they have lived for many years and which have so clearly failed to improve their economic and social situation.

Despite the fact that so large a proportion of production and income has been devoted to destructive purposes, there will be no great difficulty in repairing the material devastation, providing the social order is preserved. The modern economic system is extremely efficient in meeting a demand for commodities. We must, of course, suppose that the United States and the British Empire will be at this time leading in the task of European reconstruction, imposing sound principles of economic co-operation and realities and laying the foundations for permanent institutions of international harmony.[1]

The present war has not created any great international war debts to plague the post-war settlement. The relation between the United States and Great Britain has been resolved in very economical and ingenious fashion by the Lend-Lease Bill, which carries in its provisions a general moral for the problem of post-war transfers. Europe will, of course, need large supplies of raw materials and food; and to secure these she must have some sort of foreign credit. But we do not expect an expansion of credit such as took place in the twenties, since a reorganized world economy will be able to profit by the knowledge we have acquired of the relation between foreign debts and the exchange of goods and services as well as of the purposes which foreign credits can properly serve. Furthermore, after the period of transition, Europe will need foreign credits in any great amount only for the monetary reconstruction, as the balance of payment, exclusive of the balance of trade, should present in a longer run no tremendous difficulty; the economic possibilities of many European countries

[1] In a speech on May 29, 1941, Mr. Eden said: "It will be our wish to work with others to prevent starvation in the post-armistice period, currency disorders throughout Europe, and wide fluctuations of employment, markets, and prices, which were the cause of such misery in the twenty years between the two wars. The British Empire will actually possess, overseas, enormous stocks of food and materials which we are accumulating so as to ease the problems of overseas producers during the war and of reconstructed Europe after the war." (From the New York *Herald-Tribune*, May 30, 1941, p. 2.)

have been underestimated.¹ I shall not take up the problem of the enormous new war debts; these are in the main national debts with a low interest rate. They will present a very difficult task but one by no means impossible to achieve in an evolutionary fashion, as economic expansion is renewed.

The period of transition must see, among other projects, preparation for co-operation with Germany and the establishment of a basis for future institutional controls. Of primary importance among these will be the regulation of any measures which might be employed for the prevention of future economic aggression even in its early stage; regulation of armament production will certainly be necessary. It may also prove desirable to exclude from the process of co-operation in any important economic field (railway, post and telegraph, monetary relations, etc.) any state which alters its economy to prepare for such an aggression, as did Germany in 1933.

I do not deny that the whole is an enormous task. It can be carried out only if the great world powers co-operate, in full recognition of the world's solidarity and of their common responsibility. They have at their disposal adequate resources in the highly efficient apparatus of the modern economy. The organization must be found. A new creed, positive and optimistic, must be formulated and broadcast, expressing conviction in the dynamic forces of an expanding economy and in the free initiative and voluntary controls central to democracy. The various political, social, economic, and

---

[1] According to Cleona Lewis, *Nazi Europe and World Trade*, p. 137, European investments in 1937 in the United States amounted to $3,381,000,000 and total investments outside of Europe to $5,250,000,000. American investments in Europe came to $2,049,000,000 and total American investments abroad to $4,900,000,000 (Europe is understood here as Nazi Europe, and does not include Great Britain.)

spiritual values of human life must be co-ordinated : the necessity of discipline, of sacrifice, of duties correlative with rights, must be made obvious. The experience of the world economy in the past twenty years must be viewed not as a revolutionary alteration in all that had been before but as a step in the return to the old simple truths such as respect for basic human rights. The principle of legality must be made to prevail again, to order the proper status of men in economic life.

The defeat of the totalitarian powers which have mobilized all available forces in an effort to suppress freedom will afford the greatest possible support to believers in economic freedom. Society may truly look to the human being as its central concern, instead of to the omnipotent state in which he is only an item in a total plan. It will not be easy to organize social evolution so as to overcome the various obstacles that confront political and economic democracy. In the assembling of economic resources to meet the economic needs every country must play its proper part. Only in a co-operative policy which liberates the expanding economic forces and avoids contracting measures can the economic way out be found.

INDEX

Agricultural production, Great Britain, 74-5, 80f.; Germany, 9-10, 62, 64n; in occupied countries, 114
Appeasement, economic, 124
"Aryanization," 131f.
Autarchy, policy of, 5ff.

Barter agreements, 24f., 28ff.
Baruch, Bernard M., on priorities, 54-55
Becker, W., on German defence economy, 8
Black list, 107, 133f.
Blitzkrieg, 58, 71, 101
Blockade, 105-7, 110; Hitler on the, 6; effects altered by Germany's territorial conquests, 115f. effect of the German-Russian War on, 121
Bottlenecks, 48-49n, 54

Canada, national income and outlay (1940-41), 36n
Capitalism, and planned war economy, 38-40
Capitalistic economy, freedoms of, 14f.
Central America, blacklisting of certain firms, 133f.
Central Europe, and German foreign trade policy, 26ff., 108ff
Clearing agreements, 24f., 28ff.
Cole, G. D. H., on incomes and production, 141n
Consumers' goods, rationing of, 51f.; subsidizing, 51
Consumption, reduction of: in war economy, 35ff, 42, 48; Germany, 59ff.; Great Britain, 80; and income taxes, 44f.
Corporation tax, and war financing, 44-5

Czechoslovakia, defence preparations, 21f.; and German trade policy, 30; agreement (1940) with Poland, 146

Danubian states, 30n
Democracies, the, unpreparedness of, 17f.; reaction to Germany's economic aggression, 16-23; problem of planned war economy, 38ff., 81f.; price and wage controls in, 51f.; adjustment of production to war demands, 52; mobilization of labour and industry, 56f.; need of a constructive programme, 135; problem of economic security, 136; and free economy, 137f.
Democracy, economic, and security, 136ff.; defined, 137
Dumping, 26f.

Eccles, Marriner S., on democracy and free enterprise, 39n; on price inflation, 48n
Economic aggression, 16ff.
Economic dictatorship v. free economy, 136ff.
Emergency Powers Act (1939), 73
Ersatz. *See* Synthetic products
Europe, problems of population and area, 4-5; reaction to German economic aggression, 16-23; defence preparations, 22f.; imports (table), 118n; reconstruction, 143ff.
Excess-profits tax, and war financing, 44; Great Britain, 87n

Financing, in war economy, 41-47
Food supply, German, 10f.; Great Britain, 74; from occupied territories, 115f.

Index

Foreign trade, Germany's policy of conquest by, 23ff.; theory of declining importance of, 144f.
France, preparation for defence, 19-21
Free trade v. planned trade, 25ff.
Frechtling, Louis E., on European oil supply, 117n
Funk, Walther, on compulsory war savings, 45n

Germany, economic and social forces, 2ff.; *Lebensraum*, 4-5, 27, 127n; autarchy in, 5ff.; political and military expansion, 6f.; economic mobilization, 7ff.; pre-war food production, 8ff.; pre-war industrial production, 10ff.; raw materials, 12-14, 102, 111,; financing the defence economy, 15f.; foreign trade policy, 23ff.; imports and exports, 26f.; economic treaty (1939) with Rumania, 31; resources, compared with Great Britain's, 37f.; rationing of consumer's goods, 51; war economy, 58-71; national income, 63ff., 97n; war economy compared with Great Britain's, 94-5; imports from neutral countries, 102-3, 104; economic assets from occupied territories, 109ff.; organization of occupied territories, 111; present situation, 118f.; economic aggression met by economic appeasement, 124f.
Great Britain, preparation for defence, 19f. resources, compared with Germany's, 37f.; distribution of national income (1940), 48; system of linking wages with cost of living, 50; war economy, 71-96; economy compared with Germany's, 71, 94-5; increase in national production, 72, 77; Emergency Powers Act (1939), 73; budget, 75, 82-92; labour, 78ff.; rise in prices and wages, 79-80; national debt (1941), 89-90; ministry of economic warfare, 105; blockade, 105-9; economic problems complicated by German military successes, 109ff.; imports after the French armistice, 110f.; economic aid of the United States, 118f.
Grossraumwirtschaft, 27, 126, 135

Hardy, Charles O., on price control, 49n
Hayek, F. von, 142
Hitler, Adolf, on the blockade, 6; on the four-year plan, 8f.

Income. *See* National income; Wages
Income tax, and war financing, 44; Great Britain, 85-6
Industrial potential, decisive role of, 120; *see also* Labour; Production
Industry, in the "new order," 131f.
Inflation, defined, 42n; control of prices and incomes, 47-52; Douglas Jay on, 46n; Eccles on, 48n
Inflationary "gap," 83f.
Italy, and the blockade, 106-7

Jay, Douglas, on inflation, 46n

Kähler, Alfred, on dictatorships and armament capacities, 16
Keynes, John Maynard, 19f.; on inflationary "gap," 43
Körner, M., on economic mobilization, 7f.; quoted, 58n

Labour, and economic security, 3; mobilization of, 52-7; virtual conscription in war economy, 55; mobilization, in Germany, 61f.; mobilization, Great Britain, 78f.; in agriculture, 62, 114f.
League of Nations Stresa Conference (1932), 27; concept of aggression, 33f.
Lebensraum, 4-5, 27
Lend-Lease Bill, 38, 119, 150

Index

Little Entente, economic, 30f.
Loans and war financing, 44

Martin, John H., on priorities, 54n

National defence economy, Germany, 6ff., 15f.; democracies and, 18ff.; Great Britain, 19f.; France, 19-21
National income, control of, 47-52
Neutral countries, trade with Germany, 104; and the blockade, 106-9
"New Order," the, 126-35

Oil, European supply of, 116-18

Pigou, A. C., "real war fund," 35; on war financing by loans, 46
Poland, exports, 104n; agreement (1940) with Czechoslovakia, 146
Population and living space, 4ff.
Potential de guerre, 19
Price control, 47-52; in war economy, 39; Hardy on, 49n; Germany, 59f.; Great Britain, 72ff., 79
Prices of Goods Act (1939), 74f.
Priorities, used to regulate supply, 54f.
Production, total national, 35ff.; increase in war economy, 48f.; mobilization of, 52-6; German, increased through occupied territories, 113f.

Raw materials, German, 12-13; from occupied territories, 116
Real savings, and loans to the state, 45
Real war fund, and reduction of civilian consumption, 35ff.; increased by supplies from abroad, 37ff.; development in democracies, 38
Realwirtschaft, 6f., 15
Ritter, Carl, on German foreign trade policy, 30n
Roosevelt, Franklin D., the five freedoms, 137

Rumania, economic treaty (1939) with Germany, 31; diversion of oil from Germany, 108-9
Russia, five-year plan, 6f.; economic planning, 15; price and wage controls, 52n.; exports to Germany, 115; present situation, 121-2; importance in post-war European economy, 148f.

Savings, in German war economy, 66ff.
"Schacht Plan," 25, 29
Seas, control of, 121
South America, blacklisting of certain firms, 133f.
South-eastern Europe, trade with Germany, 28ff.
Standard of living, effect of war economy on, 37f.
Stresa Conference (1932), 27
Substitutes. *See* Synthetic products
Stock exchange, Germany, 67f.
Supply and demand, *re* stabilization through production and labour, 52ff.
Synthetic products, German manufacture of, 12f.

Taxation, and war financing, 42ff.; Germany, 64f.; Great Britain, 79, 84-5
Totalitarian states, advantage in adjustment of production to war demands, 53; adjustment of consumption, 54
Total war, democracies and, 17; economic impact of, 34ff.; financial policy in, 41-7
Transition period, from war to peacetime economy, 149-152

United Kingdom Commercial Corporation, 108
United States, defence programme, 96-100; economic aid to Great Britain, 118f.; policy of free foreign trade, 133; European investments in, 151n. *See also* Lend-Lease Bill
United States of Europe, 136, 143ff.

Unpreparedness, of democracies, 17ff.

Versailles Peace Treaty, 1

Wages, control of, 47-52; importance of stability in, 50; in Germany, 59f.; in Great Britain, 79

War, economic causes of, 1ff.

War economy, development of the "real war fund," 35ff.; total national production, 35; reduction of consumption, 36ff.; effect on standard of living, 37f.; general principles, 38-40; organization of, 40ff.; and national income, 42ff.; control of prices and incomes, 47-52; organization: mobilization of production and labour, 52-7

War financing, 41-7; by increased savings, 45f.; by loans, 44; taxation, 42ff.; Germany, 64f.; Great Britain, 75ff., 82-92

Wehrwirtschaft, and the blockade, 6-8

World economy, disruption by the World War, 2-3; German separation from, 9f., 26ff.; Stresa Conference (1932), 27; effect of German foreign trade policy on, 30f.; total war and, 126-31; solidarity of, 136

Williams, John H., on inflation, 49f.

Wriston, Henry M., on economic dictatorship, 140; on political authority in international trade, 145n.

For Product Safety Concerns and Information please contact our EU
representative GPSR@taylorandfrancis.com
Taylor & Francis Verlag GmbH, Kaufingerstraße 24, 80331 München, Germany

www.ingramcontent.com/pod-product-compliance
Lightning Source LLC
Chambersburg PA
CBHW070618300426
44113CB00010B/1577